Anatomy
of
Diplomacy

Anatomy
of
Diplomacy

The Origin and Execution of American Foreign Policy

by
Ellis Briggs

DAVID McKAY COMPANY, INC.

New York

ANATOMY OF DIPLOMACY

COPYRIGHT © 1968 BY ELLIS BRIGGS

Library of Congress Catalog Card Number: 68-18725

MANUFACTURED IN THE UNITED STATES OF AMERICA

VAN REES PRESS • NEW YORK

In the conviction that
effective diplomacy is professional diplomacy
this book is dedicated to
the men and women
of the
American Foreign Service

Contents 🖋

    lence   184

13. Push-Button Diplomacy—with a Prize for the
    Lucky Number   202

14. The Echo of the Voice of Experience   215

15. Atom Bomb versus Population Bomb, or Win-
    ner Takes Nothing   223

    Appendix   233

    Index   241

Part One:
Environment and
Ingredients

CHAPTER 1

Definitions, and How the
United States Got That Way

THE PURPOSE OF THIS BOOK IS TO RENDER MORE INTELLIGIBLE
the foreign relations of the United States. That should be
compatible with the notion that under the American system
of government, the people remain capable of comprehend-
ing their own destiny, and even at times of shaping it. The
author assumes, with occasional periods of doubt, that this
is in fact the case.

Although the struggle between dream and reality represents in a democracy an integral part of the foreign affairs
dilemma, the emphasis will be on experience and the
lessons of experience, rather than on theory. Thus professionalism will take precedence over amateurism. The crusading spirit, enrolled in a school of hard knocks, will suffer
bruises and contusions.

To promote a uniform scorecard, here are essential definitions.

By *international relations*, called interchangeably foreign
affairs and foreign relations, is meant the intercourse of
states, *through their governments*. That definition denies
the relevance of individual citizens and private groups,
whose proper recourse if they aspire to influence events

abroad is through their own governments, instead of whooping it up in foreign lands.[1]

Activity abroad by politicians is a manifestation of the cult of the busybody. It has no place in the conduct of international relations, which should be accomplished soberly and without uproar, by accredited officials representing governments. (Chapter 12 contains further observations concerning this subject.)

Diplomacy, which in a restricted sense is the art of negotiating agreements between states, has come to mean the business of conducting relations among governments. *Negotiation, representation,* and *reporting* remain the fundamental activities of professional diplomacy. The New Diplomacy [2] would add propaganda, intelligence operations, cultural osmosis, the Peace Corps, aid programs, management, and harbingers of a more abundant international life. None of them are essential. They are adjuncts to foreign relations, sometimes useful and sometimes futile, but never controlling.

When the proponents of the New Diplomacy speak disparagingly of the Old Diplomacy, they usually imply contempt for the lessons and practices of the past, plus confidence that present soothsayers have a corner on prescience, if indeed they do not know all the answers. Professors, installed in the White House cellar a few years ago, learned about these things the hard way.

In the 20th century, the *conduct* of international relations —that is to say, diplomacy—has been powerfully affected by factors that make 1914 seem almost as far from today as the American Revolution must have seemed to our grandparents in 1900. These factors include:

---

[1] The most impressive example of a private American organization that does in fact influence the conduct of foreign affairs is the Council on Foreign Relations in New York City.

[2] *I.e.,* American diplomacy since World War II.

Two devastating *world wars*, whereby the previously existing balance of power was destroyed and the United States, without adequate apprenticeship, was propelled into leadership.

The continuing *Cold War*.

Virus nationalism, which is nationalism spiked with the Tabasco sauce of xenophobia. Domestically, that is what happens to Decatur's patriotic toast "My country, right or wrong!" when it gets into the mouths of commencement orators, but in international affairs virus nationalism is the whip used by the Communists to lash backward peoples [3] into hating their former "colonial oppressors."

Goldfish bowl diplomacy, instead of open covenants, secretly arrived at.

Pyramiding *scientific achievement*, especially acceleration of communications. The airplane alone has been responsible for multiplying disorder in foreign affairs by scattering superfluous personnel over every continent and hemisphere. (Whenever anything excites the White House, inflames the Congress, or titillates the bureaucracy, supernumeraries reach for the nearest airplane and jet to the scene, to the confusion of the issues and the detriment of statesmanship. Example: the Dominican Republic, in 1965.)

At the same time that the world is shrinking, its inhabitants have shown scant capacity for matching their scientific achievements with *sociological advances*, that is, with their ability to get along with one another.

Add the *population explosion*, and the inevitable result

---

[3] Backward peoples, often primitive, are euphemistically called "undeveloped" or "underdeveloped nations," or even "emerging nations." The effect on them of virus nationalism is exacerbated by the proliferation of states, and by the doctrine of the equality of sovereignty; the ravages of these twin plagues are most spectacularly seen in the General Assembly of United Nations.

is mounting terrestrial congestion, perhaps a more sinister phenomenon than the atom bomb.

To agree that the conduct of foreign affairs has been rendered complex by the developments of the 20th century is not to concede that the traditional functions of diplomacy have been rendered obsolete, nor that negotiation, representation, and reporting have been superseded by bullhorns, Comprehensive Country Planning by Management Experts, or by the paraphernalia of the Great Society.

Turning to the raw material of foreign affairs, *national interests* are the goals and objectives of a nation. National interests reflect both the yearnings of people and the ambitions of leaders. Self-preservation, well-being and elbowroom, peace, prestige, and security are national interests. They tend to be general rather than specific, long-term rather than ephemeral.

A *foreign policy* is a course of action adopted by a Government in order to further its national interests. Foreign policy represents both implementation of a national interest and mobilization of a nation's resolution. A foreign policy is specific rather than general, and it is often comparatively short-lived.[4]

---

[4] Examples of short-lived American foreign policies:

The Stimson Doctrine, 1931 to 1933.

The Ostracize-the-Bolsheviks policy, 1919 to 1934, followed briefly by an arms-around-the-Communist-neck policy after relations had been reestablished.

A no-phony-loans-to-Latin-America policy, 1946 to 1959, followed by *Alianza para el Progreso* (1961), under which the same Good Neighbors were invited to put their hands in Uncle Sam's pocket.

The It-ain't-agonna-rain-no-more policy, exemplified by the Kellogg-Briand anti-war pact of 1929. Its demise is counted in seconds from the signing of the treaty.

A let's-boycott-perfidious-Franco policy. This was adopted with U.N. blessings in 1945. It was abandoned four years later when the unrepentant *Caudillo* proved more durable than his detractors.

Now and then a foreign policy shows remarkable survivorship stamina. The *Monroe Doctrine* was enunciated in 1823. It was still very much alive one hundred and forty-two years later, as the unruly Dominicans found out.

The *Open Door Policy*, on the other hand, lasted little more than one generation, 1899 to 1931. The purpose of the Open Door notes, maintaining Chinese integrity aside, was to guarantee that Uncle Sam could shoulder his way through any Oriental door pried open by someone else and then be on equal terms with anybody inside the pagoda. The Open Door Policy was challenged in Manchuria in 1931; at that point the United States, shaken by a depression, lacking support from the British and French, and unwilling to hazard war with Japan, backed down. The ephemeral *Stimson Doctrine* represented an effort to salvage bits and pieces of the Open Door by declining to recognize "territorial changes effected in violation of treaty obligations"—a policy ignored by the Japanese until their defeat in World War II.

The *Policy of Containment*, whereby the United States has sought since World War II to block Communist expansion, was defined in 1947 by George Kennan, a professional diplomat. That policy has been invoked by the United States on practically every continent. It is now, in Vietnam, celebrating its twenty-first anniversary. The Policy of Containment, more than any other compass, has steered the American ship of state since the collapse of President Roosevelt's Grand Design for post-Armageddon international living.

A distinguishing aspect of the foreign policy of whatever country is that it claims to be based on principles, which

---

When a *policy* becomes a *doctrine* (or vice versa) has not been established. For the purpose of this thesis, one may be used for the other.

are declared to be consonant with the national interest of
the country in question. This predilection for principles
lies at the root of more than one international dispute, since
national interests tend to overlap each other. An infatuation
for principles likewise leads to patriotic oratory, without
which few foreign policies are launched.

"Serving the vital interests of the nation" is the phrase
customarily employed at a launching.

A country's most durable policy is generally one that
serves the practical self-interest of its proponent, with a
minimum of nuisance impact on others.[5] In contrast, a
doctrine short on self-interest albeit embellished with high
moral purpose (the 1945 anti-Franco project, for instance,
or the American policy of withholding diplomatic recognition in order to undermine a regime considered objection-
able) often falls on its face almost before the accompanying
rhetoric has ceased to shake the Foggy Bottom rafters.

Other policies have been discarded because the circumstances that gave rise to them have changed. Thus "no
entangling alliances," the precept embodied in the most
influential state paper in American history, in time gave
way to NATO and SEATO and innumerable bilateral
defense pacts, any one of which had it been adopted a few
generations earlier might have made George Washington
rise up in his 18th-century grave.

Foreign policy is thus the grist in the diplomat's mill. It
is also the catnip that beguiles a Chief of State, the ragweed
that reduces his sinuses to jelly, and sometimes the booby
trap into which he may unwittingly blunder.

Foreign policy, in short, is what this book is about.

------

[5] The Monroe Doctrine met this definition throughout most of
the 19th century, during which it also enjoyed the support of the
British Navy. By 1900 the United States was sufficiently powerful
to go it alone, as Khrushchev discovered in 1962.

How the United States got that way:

A nation is the product of its environment and its history, and the United States is no exception. The colonial heritage [6] having evaporated, the American experience since independence divides itself into two eras, the ingredients of which are not difficult to identify. The first period runs from independence to the early 1900s, and the second from World War I to the present.

The first period comprises the American Revolution and the Constitution; President Washington's warning against entangling alliances; the ensuing century of vigorous territorial consolidation; the Monroe Doctrine, including its application after the Civil War to the unfortunate Maximilian in Mexico; the Spanish-American War and Manifest Destiny—down to World War I.

Twenty years after independence, Washington urged isolation from Europe, and the long peace from Waterloo to 1914 facilitated American concentration on the New World. Our emphasis throughout the 19th century was on populating a continent and subduing the land. Isolation did not apply, however, to American relations with the Far East, where Yankee missionaries and adventurers were active and successful. Clipper ships carried the American flag into as many ports of the Orient as saw the emblems of Europe. Commodore Perry visited Japan in 1854; a decade later, Alaska was purchased from Russia, and a generation after that came the annexation of Hawaii.

The 19th-century American saw little incongruous be-

---

[6] The American frontier disappeared in the 1890s. Since then the colonial heritage has sunk gradually into legend: Pocahontas, Captain Miles Standish, Rip Van Winkle, Johnny Appleseed; today the Indian yell is rarely heard outside an Ivy League football stadium.

tween no entangling alliances with Europe and aggressive behavior across the Pacific; he was too busy with the plow for overseas preoccupations. When, about 1900, American citizens did wake up to foreign affairs, the whiffs of world power produced not distemper, but euphoria. Manifest Destiny, with its garland of colonies plucked from Spain, plus a flamboyant President with a penchant for foreign adventure, combined to render the early years of the 20th century a happy and carefree period.

It was exhilarating to flex our international muscles. It was fun to police the Caribbean and to build a Panama Canal, to free Cuba and to promise freedom to the Philippines, to mediate the Russo-Japanese War, and to send an American fleet around the globe for all the world to see. In our newly discovered strength it was splendid to be a Great Power and to exchange cadenced amenities with other Great Powers—nations bent like ourselves upon preserving the best of all possible worlds.

These eupeptic contemplations were shattered by World War I, and things have never been the same since.

The second era of American experience runs from 1914 to the present. In two world wars, we have witnessed unparalleled destruction and suffering, the afterpain of which pursues us. We have seen the decline of the countries of Western Europe, their commonwealths disintegrated and their inhabitants bewildered and resentful. We have seen the spawning of countless succession states, few of them viable, and we have seen the birth and growth of Communist imperialism, an ugly wave still churning our beaches.

The era has seen two world organizations, the League of Nations and United Nations, each powerless to keep the peace, but each representing mankind's hope for a future based on justice derived from acceptance of law. It has seen matchless progress in material things, with lack of birth control threatening to wipe out that progress. And it has seen man probing space, but in peril of destroying himself on earth by the misuse of forces which, if harnessed to production, could provide incalculable blessings.

As this juggernaut of contradictions gained momentum after the outbreak of World War I, the United States, a latecomer to the international grandstand, was confused and confounded by what it saw.

At first we found the conflict incredible, and we pretended it wasn't so. We pretended that "the war will be over by Christmas" (Christmas of 1914), and then that we ourselves were "too proud to fight," and then again that we fought "to make the world safe for democracy."

Undevastated America pretended in 1918 that its allies had not been bled white in victory, the next year at Versailles that a peace of vengeance would be enforceable, and in 1920 that that peace was iniquitous and that the League of Nations would impair United States sovereignty. The American people pretended that "back to normalcy" was a truer motto than "the moving finger writes," that Prohibition would strengthen our moral character, and that a chicken in every pot would cure the Depression. We even pretended that Communist Russia could never learn to fix the plumbing.

Meanwhile, the discredited German Kaiser, widely blamed for unleashing World War I, had been replaced by Adolf Hitler and his Nazis, who were infinitely worse. Mussolini was making the Italian trains run on time. And Japan, having outfaced the United States, went methodically about the business of dominating Asia. Franklin Roosevelt's Good Neighbor Policy, one of the few bright things in the dismal 1930s, had little impact outside the New World.

It was in 1941 at Pearl Harbor that the United States

was finally forced to come to grips with the responsibilities of leadership. Since World War II, that leadership has involved the American people in constant and at times frenetic activity, all over the world.

The Marshall Plan, which rebuilt Western Europe.

The Truman Plan, which saved Greece and Turkey from going the way of Bulgaria and Rumania.

The North Atlantic Alliance, greatest accomplishment of the early postwar period. NATO provided not only security, but the confidence without which European political stability could not have been reestablished, nor economic growth resumed.

The Korean War, undertaken for good and sufficient reasons, but stymied in deference to timid allies, dissension at home, and United Nations mythology.

Successor to the Korean stalemate is the current struggle in Southeast Asia.

Not to forget over one hundred billion dollars in American aid programs, the efforts to promote and stabilize international trade, atoms-for-peace, the space program, Alliance for Progress, and the politically popular Peace Corps.

Any catalog of these operations is impressive. In broadest context they are the American attempts to adjust to a changed and still rapidly changing world, in which the possession of strength has not always been synonymous with the ability to apply it successfully, and in which the existence of good intentions has not been a guarantee that even our friends would take those intentions for granted.

In narrower context, those postwar operations represent the American answer to Communist expansion. And if it is objected that containment is a negative thing, that Communism has yet to disgorge the first acre of looted territory, and that there have been defeats as well as victories—in short, that the struggle continues, and that Communism is still dedicated to our destruction—nevertheless, containment does represent an achievement that should not be belittled because of the dimensions of the tasks ahead.

Recognizing the negative aspects of containment, a search for more positive goals, consistent with individual freedom, has likewise gone forward. Wanted: something to appeal to mature and developed nations and at the same time arouse the interest of the emerging nations—the new states of Africa, for instance.

The preliminary results are not lacking in irony. The most popular alternative to Communism that the leaders of the free world have thus far been able to recommend is the Welfare State, which is called this or that in various places—at the moment in the United States, the Great Society.

Historians describe the Welfare State as a game that eventually bankrupts the players. Its trademark is the never-balanced national budget, and its product is inflation, a thief with his hand on everyman's pocketbook. Of all the lessons endorsed by experience, none is more significant than the lesson that when self-reliance is replaced by reliance upon Government, then Easy Street becomes Dead-end Street, and civilization is facing a time of trouble.

It is with these and related problems, as well as with the physical containment of Communism, that the United States has been trying to cope ever since World War II ended. As the bicentennial of American independence approaches, the contrasts between what the original thirteen colonies sought from Britain, and what the hypnotists of the Great Society are peddling beside the Potomac are sufficiently startling, but in terms of foreign affairs, that need not unduly complicate our review.

Let us examine, instead, how foreign policy is made.

CHAPTER 2

The Presidency and
Foreign Affairs

IN THE UNITED STATES, THE PRESIDENT MAKES AND THE
President executes foreign policy. For anyone in a hurry,
that is all he has to read of this chapter.

The Executive does not, however, possess exclusive jurisdiction over foreign affairs. By dividing responsibility between the President and the legislature, the Constitution [1]
started a tug of war that is as old as the republic. But it is
an unequal contest. As Chief Executive, as Commander in
Chief, as treaty-maker and as arbiter of personnel, it is the
President who, when the rope is taut, gives the decisive pull.

There are additional reasons for Presidential ascendancy.
By controlling official communications, the President is
better informed than the Congress about foreign events
and, equally important, he is informed first. By being able
through the utilization of military forces to commit the

---

[1] Authority over foreign affairs derives principally from Articles
One and Two of the Constitution. Article Two, Section 1, vests the
Executive Power in the President; and Section 2, Paragraph 1, provides that the President shall be commander in chief of the armed
forces. Paragraph 2 of Section 2 covers treaties and appointments,
except recess appointments, which are in Paragraph 3.
Money bills, and the enactment of laws and resolutions, are
dealt with in Article One, Section 7.

prestige of the United States, a President can usurp the war-making power of the Congress. Furthermore, because of greatly increased American Government operations abroad during the last quarter-century, not only has the President become more active in foreign affairs, but the power of the Presidency has risen, while that of the legislature has declined. That is a trend to which the Congress, and especially the Senate, remains unreconciled, but it is a fact that when the international chips are down, the President usually does the calling.

That does not mean that Congressional participation in foreign affairs is a rubber-stamp business—far from it! Congressional activity has powerfully influenced events in the past, and will undoubtedly continue to do so. The shared powers include Senatorial advice-and-consent on ratification of treaties and on Presidential appointments, as well as the power of the purse, exercised initially by the House and then by both chambers. Those powers are never unimportant, and Congressional prerogatives are jealously maintained.

Congressional powers are discussed in the next chapter.

To facilitate his foreign policy operations, the President has an abundant reservoir of talent, beginning with the State Department and its secular arm, the Foreign Service, plus a plethora of other executive departments and agencies, each with a real or imagined justification for participating, and most of them eager to get into the diplomatic picture. This crowding and shoving of the supernumeraries complicates matters, and sometimes (as during the Franklin Roosevelt Administration) it practically paralyzes them.

To ride herd on the mavericks, as well as to try to keep a semblance of order on the range, the White House now has a Special Assistant for Foreign Affairs, theoretically versed in those mysteries, and two powerful institutions, the Budget Bureau and the National Security Council, attached to his Office.

These accretions are comparatively recent. The Assistant dates from 1939, but he did not acquire self-propelled roller skates until the present decade. The Budget Bureau was transferred to the White House from Treasury as World War II approached, and it now occupies the old State War Navy Building, next door to 1600 Pennsylvania Avenue. The Bureau derives its influence from the fact that no departmental appropriation request can reach the President's desk until Budget has approved it. Since foreign relations activities, microscopic in cost compared to defense expenditures or putting a rocket in orbit, nevertheless do involve money, the State Department must first convince the Budget Bureau that it needs an extra Amharic-speaking Vice Consul in Addis Ababa. To debate the alleged importance of sending the Vice Consul to Ethiopia, as well as to consider broader and more important aspects of State Department living, Budget maintains a considerable staff of its own foreign affairs specialists, each eager to get a finger into diplomacy.

The National Security Council was established in 1947, and its mandate is "to advise the President with respect to the integration of domestic, foreign and military policies relating to the national security...," clearly a license to hunt in any cover from Florida to Alaska, plus the whole wide world outside American territory. The NSC has a formidable membership, including the President and Vice President and the Secretaries of State and Defense. The Secretary of the Treasury, the Chairman of the Joint Chiefs of Staff, and the Director of the Central Intelligence Agency (which agency is a creature of the NSC) likewise attend, together with such other ranking officials as the agenda of a given session may indicate.

The National Security Council broods about Long Range

Goals (future policy) and also about Crisis Situations. Because of too abundant raw material in the crisis category, much of its time has been devoted to fire fighting: the unedifying U-2 pother and its aftermath of torpedoed summitry, the Bay of Pigs disaster, the confrontation with Khrushchev over missiles in Cuba, Dominican intervention, and the escalated war in Vietnam—to mention items recently engaging NSC attention.

Until the advent of the Kennedy Administration (1961) the National Security Council possessed, in addition, an active dependency called the Operations Coordinating Board, the ostensible responsibility of which was to see to it that the decisions of the President, issued via the National Security Council, were properly implemented. Instead, the Operations Coordinating Board recruited and multiplied itself; it grew larger and larger. Soon it was acting with respect to senior departments and agencies like a suspicious and somewhat hostile power. One of President Kennedy's first acts after taking the oath of office was to eliminate the Operations Coordinating Board, but thereupon—instead of waiting for the insecticide to settle—Kennedy filled the premises with professors.

Let us examine how some of our 20th-century Presidents have discharged their responsibilities toward foreign affairs.

Theodore Roosevelt (1901 to 1909) sailed close to the Constitutional wind, and sometimes when there was practically no wind to sail by. He was the happy extrovert, the end-justifies-the-means President, who always preferred doing something to nothing. Roosevelt was suited to the mood of the United States at the turn of the century, and to the status of the nation as a recently emerged Great Power.

It was Roosevelt who adopted the corollary to the Monroe Doctrine, making the United States the constable of the Caribbean: it was he who fomented a banana revo-

lution for the greater good of world trade across a pesti-
lential isthmus and who set Cuba free—subject to an apron
string tied to mythical good behavior. Farther afield, Roosevelt intervened successfully in the Russo-Japanese War,
knocking heads together at a peace conference in New
Hampshire and blithely selling Korea down the Yalu River.
He participated in the Algeciras Conference—primarily
because the other big boys were there—and in 1906 he sent
the Great White Fleet around the world. When Congress
threatened to withhold funds, President Roosevelt, ascertaining that the Navy Department had enough coal to go
halfway around, left it to Congress to get the ships back
home again.

After enjoying every moment of eight years in office,
Roosevelt departed from Washington to chase lions in
Africa, leaving the genial Taft to soften the echoes along
the Potomac.

Woodrow Wilson (1913 to 1920) was another foreign
affairs do-it-yourself President, but for different reasons.
Burdened for two years by the most inept Secretary of
State on record,[2] who resigned because he found the mild
Lusitania note too stiff, Wilson was for six years thereafter
in effect his own foreign minister, to his Versailles undoing.
Reelected in 1916 on the slogan "He kept us out of war,"
six months later [3] he led the country into the conflict, and
on to victory "to make the world safe for democracy."

Wilson's Fourteen Points read well today,[4] and his appeal
for "a general association of nations . . . formed . . . for the
purpose of affording mutual guarantees of political inde-

---

[2] A runner-up repainted the State Department doors in the 1940s.
[3] In April 1917, after Germany resumed unrestricted submarine
sinkings.
[4] Except the first one, advocating "open covenants . . . openly
arrived at," the impracticality of which Wilson himself recognized
during the Versailles Conference in 1919.

pendence and territorial integrity to great and small states alike" was an eloquent plea for American participation in a world organization—a plea rejected by the Senate less than two years later. The rejection, however, was not so much repudiation of international collaboration as it was of Wilsonian inflexibility. Because as a politician he remained the articulate amateur, never learning that statesmanship must combine with its vision the ability to accomplish, Wilson lost his battle with the Senate. For all his soaring inspiration of a better world, that was Wilson's tragedy.

Franklin Roosevelt (1933 to 1945), the poorest administrator to occupy the White House, played foreign affairs loudly, but by ear. He distrusted and bypassed his own State Department, and he peppered the international scene with Special Representatives and Coordinators, who produced mainly confusion. In leading the nation out of a depression, in preparing the country for war and converting it into an "arsenal for democracy," and as wartime helmsman of the ship of state, Roosevelt showed leadership, courage, and imagination, but his record is marred by miscalculations, exuberantly arrived at.

Roosevelt's handling of the London Economic Conference in 1933 [5] was a prototype of ineptitude. His insistence on the unconditional surrender of Germany prolonged the war in Europe.[6] And his optimistic hallucination that "I can do business with Uncle Joe" helped hatch the problems that plague the world today, more than two decades after his death.[7]

---

[5] *Cf. 1933, Characters in Crisis* by Dr. Herbert Feis.

[6] After Roosevelt's death, the unconditional surrender mistake was not repeated with Japan, thanks to the representations of former Ambassador Joseph Grew.

[7] E.g., the isolation of Berlin, the division of Germany, the betrayal of Poland, and the establishment of satellites in eastern Europe.

Harry Truman (1945 to 1953) was the inheritor—first of victory and then of its problems. His was the task of finding perches for chickens coming home to roost, and as World War II ground to a halt, the skies were dark with them.

Starting with so little, rarely has one man accomplished so much. Completing the unfinished task of Woodrow Wilson, Truman presided over the establishment of United Nations. Without flinching he faced the decision of the atom bomb, and with equal fortitude the Cold War. He revitalized Europe (the Marshall Plan) and he saved Greece and Turkey (the Truman Plan). Truman forged the NATO alliance, and he gave his name to the Point Four program for sharing with others the technical skills of the United States. With four successive Secretaries of State, in ascending order of competence, Truman rescued the transaction of the foreign business of the United States from the disorders of the preceding twelve years.

Only in Korea did President Truman falter. After committing American troops to repel Communist aggression, thus joining the grim issue in Asia, Truman accepted the stalemate his successor ratified as the Korean armistice. That unfinished business led ten years later to Vietnam.

The popular Dwight Eisenhower (1953 to 1961) did not in spite of honesty and goodwill live up to the promise of his popularity.[8] At the outset of his administration, the failure to cope with the unclean Senator McCarthy damaged American prestige abroad beyond the power of partisan propaganda to repair.

A strong Secretary of State (Dulles) kept the propeller turning and the international pot boiling, but in spite of exhortations and defense pacts, there was more steam than

---

[8] See *The Ordeal of Power* by Emmet Hughes. (New York: Atheneum, 1963.)

casserole, and more mileage than solid accomplishment. Meanwhile, Eisenhower's penchant for summitry was even more unprofitable. The Spirit of Camp David, hailed as a triumph of face-to-face diplomacy, did not survive the U-2 fiasco; a meeting of Latin American Presidents, initiated by Eisenhower, approached the ultimate in futility; and a Far East junket ended in greater humiliation than any American President has experienced abroad. Personable and impressive as Chief of State, as head of government Eisenhower rarely did his homework.

The thousand days of John Kennedy (1961 to 1963) were enough to mark him as a President undaunted by the exercise of his Constitutional responsibilities, who did do his homework, and who profited by experience, from the mortification of the Bay of Pigs to the triumph the following year over Soviet missiles in Castro's Cuba. Graceful of phrase and articulate of expression, Kennedy apparently cherished to his death the hope that if sufficient intellectual heat could be generated,[9] a problem would disintegrate, or at the least become malleable. The fact that his own galvanic battery worked overtime may have encouraged that presumption which, whatever its merits in science, seems of doubtful relevance in foreign affairs.

Reportedly impatient with the State Department for not producing butterflies-on-demand, it will not now be known whether Kennedy would eventually have fumigated the White House of the larval Secretaries of State he attracted, or whether he would have continued indefinitely to operate a private State Department from a White House clothes closet. It is of interest, however, that one of his early foreign affairs directives was a message (May 1961) to American Ambassadors abroad, redefining and clarifying their respon-

---

[9] *Cf.* President Truman's "If you can't stand the heat, get out of the kitchen."

sibilities and confirming them in the authority required for effective performance.[10] That attitude could have been equally germane to the State Department.

It was Lyndon Johnson (1963 . . .) who, in the heat of Vietnam and in the midst of other foreign and domestic preoccupations, returned to the Department of State the "overall direction, coordination and supervision" of American Government activities overseas. This formidable assignment—the counterpart of Kennedy's reaffirmation of the primacy of the Ambassador abroad—is recorded as National Security Action Memorandum 341 of March 4, 1966, and it is of interest to note that the principal architect of the directive was not the Secretary of State, but a professional military man—a former Chairman of the Joint Chiefs of Staff.[11]

It remains to be seen how this historic challenge will be met by the inhabitants of Foggy Bottom, who time and again since the Franklin Roosevelt Administration have seen the State Department challenged as the agency primarily responsible, under the President, for international relations. Theirs is at long last the opportunity to put foreign affairs into comprehensible and more orderly channels, but implementation of the new order will affect the activities of countless bureaus and officials with interests abroad, who may now be required to forgo the exhilaration of free-wheeling across the hitherto unfenced world scene.

---

[10] This excellent directive is the most useful document issued by a President to American Ambassadors since World War II. It confirms the Ambassador, the personal representative of the President, as the senior United States official in the country concerned (except in war areas), and it makes the Ambassador responsible for the success of the entire government operations—or accountable for its failure.

The text is printed in the Appendix.

[11] General Maxwell D. Taylor, later Ambassador to Vietnam.

Their response to the order has yet to be recorded, but the State Department record since 1966 is far from impressive.

As the foregoing summaries indicate, the enormous authority of the President under the Constitution has been utilized in this century in a wide variety of forms and directions. Presidential power—diplomatic, economic, and military—has on occasion been applied or withheld, dispersed or canalized, concentrated in the White House or delegated to trusted associates, depending on the way in which the Chief Executive himself has interpreted successive problems in the light of his responsibilities and the country's estimated resources.

In the nature of its ingredients, diplomacy is an imprecise craft.[12] That is bound to be so; the variants in even the least complex international situation can rarely be plotted until after the event. This inherent uncertainty perhaps explains why so many spectators of foreign affairs aspire to be players, and why so many kibitzers volunteer to be coaches. Furthermore, because some of the most difficult international dilemmas remain insoluble, the temptation to im-

---

[12] "Foreign affairs is a complicated and disorderly business, full of surprises, demanding hard choices that must often be based on judgment rather than analysis, involving relations with more than a hundred countries diverse in their traditions and political institutions—all taking place in a world that changes so rapidly that memory and experience are quickly out of date. Coordination, integration, and rational management are surely desirable; but whether it is humanly possible to meet anything more than the barest minimum standards is a question to which an optimistic answer can be based only on faith." From the opening paragraph of a Memorandum prepared by Dr. Thomas C. Schelling, Professor in the Faculty of Public Administration at Harvard University, at the request of the Subcommittee on National Security and International Operations of the Committee on Government Operations of the United States Senate. (The so-called Jackson Subcommittee). U.S. Government Printing Office, 1968.

provise lurks forever in the background, dangerous and beguiling. The possessor of power is thus encouraged to believe he can dream up the answers.

President Johnson's directive of 1966 to the Department of State is not, of course, the first example of delegation of authority over foreign relations by a Chief Executive. During the period under review, the actions of President Harding with respect to Secretary of State Hughes, of Hoover to Stimson, of Truman to Marshall and later to Acheson, and of Eisenhower to Dulles, can all be cited.

It is important to recognize, however, that never before NSAM-341 has the delegation of authority for the conduct of foreign affairs been in such specific and comprehensive terms. Never before has a Secretary of State been assigned "authority and responsibility ... for the overall direction, coordination and supervision of interdepartmental activities of the United States Government overseas."

The directive is an outgrowth of studies undertaken in 1961, following the Bay of Pigs experience, when a group was formed by President Kennedy to appraise that unhappy episode and to seek to identify the organizational deficiencies that permitted it to happen. Following that investigation and several years of additional study, it was concluded that the analogy of the Ambassador and his "Country Team" abroad, whereby the chief of diplomatic mission is made responsible for the entire effort of all the agencies of our Government in a given country, could usefully be employed with reference to the Department of State and the other departments and agencies concerned with aspects of international affairs in the national capital.

The mechanics adopted are sufficiently simple and uncumbersome to give some promise of success, always provided that State accepts the challenge: there is established one Senior Interdepartmental Group, under the chairmanship of the Under Secretary of State, and beneath it five Interdepartmental Regional Groups, under the chairmanship respectively of the Assistant Secretaries of State for European, Latin American, African, Near and Middle East, and Far Eastern Affairs. At the same time, in accordance with recommendations contained in the Herter Committee report of 1962, and endorsed by Secretary Rusk, the State Department has set about upgrading (as the bureaucratic word has it) the so-called Country Desk Officers. They are the officials who henceforth will in the first instance call the turns that affect successive countries with which the United States maintains relations.[13]

All of which is challenging, and potentially of the highest importance. But no scheme, no plan, no delegation of authority can be more successful than the Chief Executive who orders it, who then must support it in terms of day-to-day operations. Faced with the magnitude of foreign affairs tasks, their urgency, and their mounting complexity, the Presidency remains—as ex-Presidents themselves have declared—a frightening and well-nigh overwhelming *individual* job. Nothing, literally nothing, can be substituted for the decision of the lonely man who occupies the White House.

---

[13] The only foreign affairs activities excluded from the foregoing allocation of responsibility are military operations, which the President as Commander in Chief continues to direct through the channel of command via the Department of Defense and the Joint Chiefs of Staff to overseas commanders.

CHAPTER 3

The Role of Congress in
Foreign Affairs 🪶

THE INFLUENCE OF CONGRESS IN FOREIGN AFFAIRS IS SUB-
ordinate to that of the President. Nevertheless, because of
participation in *treaty-making* and *appointments,* and because of power over the *purse,* Congressional influence will
always be great. There has in addition been increased activity in a fourth field of Congressional interest, that of
surveillance over Executive operations. That is the Congressional function of scrutiny, investigation and review, as
described hereafter.

Treaties cannot be ratified by the President until the
"advice and consent" of the Senate have been obtained.
The most famous treaty case occurred in 1919 when the
Senate rejected the Versailles Treaty and the League of
Nations—a step which profoundly affected American foreign
relations between the two world wars. The underlying
reason for rejection was skepticism over the impact of
internationalism on the sovereignty of the United States,
but the immediate reason was the hostility of the Foreign
Relations Committee and its Chairman, Henry Cabot

Lodge, toward President Wilson, who had invited no Senators to accompany him to Paris.[1]

Internationalists are fond of proclaiming that if the Senate had approved the League of Nations, American participation could have postponed and might even have avoided World War II. Maybe so; that can never be proved. Rejection of the treaty did destroy President Wilson, and it gave an isolationist bent to American diplomacy for several years thereafter.

Another Senate treaty action that bore heavily on our international relations—this time with Latin America—was the imposition on Cuba of the Platt Amendment, which legalized interventions deemed in Washington to be for the good of the Cuban people.[2]

Cuba embodied the Platt Amendment in its constitution rather than further delay independence, but at heart the Cuban people never accepted it. Nor did their Latin American cousins, who at succeeding Pan American conferences did their utmost to make "intervention" an ugly word, embarrassing to the United States.

Recognizing the anachronism of the servitude imposed on Cuba, as well as the vulnerability of the United States to Cuban plotting aimed precisely at producing American intervention, the United States by treaty in 1934 abrogated the Platt Amendment, amid hemisphere rejoicing. (One vestige remains, the Guantánamo Naval Station, regularly denounced by Fidel Castro.)

The Senate can also *delay* treaties, there being no pro-

---

[1] Forty-three years after Senate rejection of the Versailles Treaty, partisanship went full circle with the appointment by Democratic Presidents Kennedy and Johnson of Lodge's son, himself a former Republican Senator, to be Ambassador to Vietnam.

[2] In this instance, in contrast to its League of Nations veto, the Senate acted in agreement with the Theodore Roosevelt Administration.

vision in the Constitution requiring action within a specified period. Another Cuban case comes to mind in that connection—the treaty returning the Isle of Pines. Senate
action was withheld for nearly a quarter of a century, in
deference to the American grapefruit growers on the island,
who feared the effect of the United States tariff if the
territory went back to Cuban jurisdiction.[3]

Again, by not acting on the Soviet consular convention of
1964, the Senate blocked for three years the granting of
diplomatic immunity to an enlarged quota of Russian
consular officials in the United States (to the satisfaction
of the Federal Bureau of Investigation). That inaction
simultaneously delayed the extension of less unfavorable
treatment of private American citizens who run afoul of
Communist justice in the Soviet Union (to the distress of
the Department of State).

Two unrelated practices have flowed from recognition
by the Executive of the power of the Senate over treaties.
Mindful of President Wilson's League of Nations debacle,
subsequent Presidents have sought to render important
treaties partnership operations between the Executive and
the Senate. This has been accomplished by such devices as
advance and continuing consultation with key Senators,
and the inclusion of important Senate members on American delegations appointed to negotiate.

Thus the Dumbarton Oaks and San Francisco Conferences, which drafted the Charter of United Nations,
received important contributions from Senatorial negotiators, and unlike the Covenant of the League, the Charter

---

[3] When the Senate finally gave its advice and consent to ratification of the Isle of Pines treaty, the grapefruit growers, true to their
pessimistic prediction, went broke. They sold their orchards to
Japanese farmers whose presence on the Isle of Pines, slingshots
aimed at the Panama Canal, caused sharp twinges of apprehension
in Washington after Pearl Harbor.

passed the Senate with ease. And the NATO alliance of the Democratic Truman Administration was preceded by a Senate Resolution in which the Republican Vandenberg played a leading part; the Resolution constituted advance approval by the Senate of the NATO treaty commitment.

The other development is the Executive Agreement, an instrument not requiring submission to the Senate, which Congress accepted on the theory that in each case the policy involved would already have been approved by the legislature. Status-of-forces agreements governing the rights and immunities of American troops serving in Allied countries, and agreements negotiated pursuant to the Trade Agreements Act, are examples of Executive Agreements, literally hundreds of which have gone into effect during the past thirty years, at a vast saving of time and effort for the Government.

The Senate likewise takes seriously its powers with respect to Presidential *appointments*. Although the great majority of those in the foreign affairs field, including career Foreign Service appointments, are promptly endorsed, Presidential nominations are always scrutinized, not infrequently debated, and occasionally rejected.

For example, shortly after World War II, the Senate declined to act on President Truman's nomination of General Mark Wayne Clark to be Ambassador to the Vatican. The Senate had nothing against the nominee, but it took exception to establishing diplomatic relations with the Catholic Church—a project which it blocked by not confirming Clark's nomination.[4]

---

[4] President Truman eventually withdrew the nomination and the State Department, in a burst of generosity, reimbursed the General for a civilian wardrobe, including the opulent pinafore in which he had expected to present his credentials to the Pope. Clark terminated his official career not as a diplomat, but as Commanding General in Korea.

Similarly, by pocketing the nominations, the Senate in 1966 thwarted the effort of State Department administrators to enlarge the Foreign Service by the blanket induction of eight hundred propagandists from the United States Information Agency. The Committee on Foreign Relations declined to act on these nominations, and that ended the matter.

In the controversial-nominee category may also be mentioned Admiral Straus, an Eisenhower candidate for Chairman of the Atomic Energy Commission, who was rejected by the Senate; and Mrs. Clare Boothe Luce, nominated in 1959 to be Ambassador to Brazil, who after spirited debate was confirmed.

The importance of power over the *purse* is self-evident. It renders the Committee on Appropriations of the House, where money bills originate, far more influential in foreign matters than the Foreign Affairs Committee, which unlike its Senate counterpart has no role in either treaties or appointments. In fact, the purse power permits one subcommittee chairman, with few constituents versed in diplomacy and little comprehension of foreign policy, regularly to bleed the State Department budget and to keep American representation abroad on short rations.

Another device employed by the House of Representatives is the insertion in an appropriation bill of a provision that specified funds shall not be utilized in a certain way. For instance, in 1965 the President of Egypt, a free-food pensioner of the United States, publicly denounced his benefactor. This occurred at a time when, of over four

---

Nowadays, when a President wants to communicate with the Vatican, he usually does so through the American Embassy in Rome, or if he wishes sirens and publicity, by sending to Vatican City the American Ambassador to United Nations—an Abie's Irish Rose gambit that rarely fails to stimulate the parishioners.

hundred million dollars' worth of "food for peace" earmarked for Egypt, approximately seventy-five million dollars' worth still remained to be shipped to the Nile. Discovering this, the House of Representatives voted to curtail further deliveries. They probably reasoned that relieving Nasser of the necessity of buying food for his teeming *fellaheen* might release equivalent funds for him to devote to mischief-making in the Near East. However, what the legislators in effect were seeking was to substitute their judgment of what would best serve American foreign policy interests for the judgment of the Chief Executive. The House of Representatives sought, that is, to limit the power of the President.

Thus the tug-of-war between the Congress and the Executive continues.[5]

The role of Congress in cases of this nature will be identified as essentially *negative*: the President should not do this, or the President must not spend the taxpayers' appropriated

---

[5] In a struggle of the character described, the President usually takes the position that the proposed Congressional action would be an impairment of the flexibility needed by the Chief Executive for his day-to-day conduct of international relations in a fast-changing world. White House political resources are then mobilized—in the Senate, for instance—and the upshot in a given case is often a compromise which, while dealing with the restriction in question, acknowledges the right of Congress to limit Presidential action. In the Egyptian case, Nasser eventually got his wheat, apparently on the theory that the presumed goodwill of the hungry *fellaheen* outweighed the dictator's nuisance value. (This seems, after the event, to be a debatable solution.)

It is of interest to record also that during the last two decades of American largesse the Congress, while appropriating many billions of dollars for foreign aid, has shown more interest in promoting minimum standards of conduct on the part of the alien beneficiaries than the Chief Executive, citing "impaired flexibility," has been willing to tolerate.

Since the Guarani Indians do not vote in American Congressional elections, this is a puzzling phenomenon.

money on that. This negative performance explains much
of the legislative unease over its foreign affairs participation.
Congress legitimizes or amends or restricts policies and
actions initiated by the Chief Executive, rather than itself
initiating them.

Many Congressman find this situation frustrating; they
believe it should be the other way around. Dissatisfied with
their international contribution, they seek to enlarge it—an
aspiration nourished by lack of precision in the Constitution itself. This has led to expanded activity in the fourth
and final field of Congressional activity—the scrutiny, investigation, and review of Executive operations—in a word,
Congressional *surveillance*.

Because nowadays almost anything undertaken by the
United States has some foreign relations relevance—military
activities, disarmament, atomic experiments, food, world
health, population control, whaling, international finance,
the tourist trade, or whatever—almost anything that Congress elects to investigate can be represented as relating to
foreign policy. Congress has so represented, and this insistence has led to three important postwar developments
affecting the State Department.

The first is the increased competence of the permanent
professional staffs of Congressional committees. Without
their knowledgeable and painstaking work, much Congressional study would be haphazard or useless.[6]

The second is the increasing demand on the time of the
Secretary of State and his ranking subordinates, represented

---

[6] Cases in point are the Foreign Relations Committee of the
Senate, and the subcommittee on Government Operations under
Senator Jackson. A danger exists that such committees may end by
establishing their own "foreign offices," complete with regional
experts, proliferation, and bureaucracy, and that these will try to
compete with the Department of State.

by Congressional summons to appear before committees and testify, which in fact means *to attempt to justify* this or that aspect of international policy. Perhaps recent Secretaries have not taken to living aboard airplanes to escape this form of legislative inquisition, but there is no denying that the power to require testimony has been abused since the war. Today it seriously handicaps the performance of responsible officials.

The third development is Congressional travel abroad, which has reached almost astronomical proportions, with the result that at some of the more "popular" foreign capitals, the care and feeding of itinerant Congressmen has become the principal business occupying American Embassies during several months of each year.[7]

On net balance the three developments cited are probably beneficial. A well-staffed Congressional committee is a more efficient committee, and one more likely to be sympathetic to the legitimate needs of diplomacy. The power of investigation and review can keep a bureaucracy on its toes, even though an inordinate amount of the time of

---

[7] That is a circumstance not necessarily unattractive to traveling legislators, whose view of the proficiency of American diplomacy can be affected by duty-free bourbon and cigarettes, access to post exchanges, twelve-hour laundry service, or the confection of short-order suits in Hong Kong—as well as Chancery briefings on the intricacies of tribal politics in Nigeria, or the relationship of the Inner Six to the Outer Seven in Europe.

At the author's last post, definitely a "popular" capital, a twenty-four-hour watch was maintained at the international airport specifically for the purpose of meeting and greeting legislators, verifying their local hotel accommodations and transporting them thither, and furnishing them with local currency, guides, addresses, or whatnot. This involved the assignment of three English-speaking local employees and one Government-owned sedan; in terms of the peace of mind of the American Ambassador, who otherwise would have been aroused from sleep six nights out of seven, never was the taxpayers' money better spent!

State Department officials is spent in Congressional corridors and antechambers, waiting for hearings to take place. And something useful possibly rubs off on even the most frivolous Congressional traveler—in contrast to whom a substantial proportion of visiting legislators engage in serious study and in genuine efforts to broaden their understanding of United States interests abroad.

Notwithstanding, however, the best efforts of the Executive and his diplomatic agents, the attitude of Congress toward the Department of State is rarely cordial and often embittered. No single agency of the Government has been so frequently assailed or so harshly criticized by the legislature as the embattled guardians of the peace, ensconced these last twenty years behind their ugly barricades in Foggy Bottom.

The roots of Congressional antipathy are deep, and of long standing. Legislators represent "the people." They suspect what has to do with "the elite"; among foreigners, diplomacy was long the province of the aristocracy, and hence is regarded as a suitable subject for attack by the champions of democracy. Identification of "elite" with "undemocratic" also nourishes the fable that "American boys are no match for the wily foreigners," which phrase is the progenitor of the equally silly legend "We never lost a war or won a peace."

Again, isolation and "no entangling alliances" may have been buried in twin graves at the turn of the century, but their ghosts remain with us, handy and convenient emanations for a Congressman to conjure up for domestic political purposes, in the advancement of which it is the State Department that sometimes gets spooked by the ghosts.

Then, too, since World War II the American Government has involved itself abroad in all sorts of operational activities and adventures, many of dubious value and others

initiated with flamboyant promises impossible of fulfillment: all those costly aid programs, tutelage of "emerging
nations," Food for Peace, and the boys and girls of the
Peace Corps busy fumigating this and supervising that.
Never in history have so many neighborhoods been invaded
by so many people trying to accomplish so much with so
little previous experience.

Not all of these undertakings could possibly be conducted efficiently. When irregularities have occurred, or a
program has bogged down, or a beneficiary has spit in the
benefactor's eye, it is the Congressional custom to blame
the Department of State, even though few projects were
operated under State Department jurisdiction, and many
were launched over State Department objection. (As noted
in the previous chapter, in 1966 the State Department became responsible for the first time for Government operations abroad, except military operations.)

Most important of all, however, in terms of Congressional relations with the State Department, the foreign
affairs of the United States have not since the end of
World War II been uniformly prosperous. In the nature of
the Cold War, they probably could not be. But in those
circumstances it has proved convenient for the Congress
to have a scapegoat to blame for such setbacks as the "loss
of China," or continuing Communist aggression, or Cuba,
or the drift toward dictatorship in Africa and Latin
America. The Department of State, with no Washington
lobby, no constituency to wound, and no megaphone to
shout back through, makes in the eyes of many legislators
the ideal target whenever a miscalculation has been made,
or a toe has been stubbed, or a brickbat is there to be
thrown.

The question arises whether the relations between State
and Congress could not be improved and whether, granted

the importance of having the foreign affairs mechanism work as smoothly as possible, further efforts ought not to be put forth. The answer is that such efforts are in fact being made, on a continuing basis.

Until 1949 the State Department lacked a Congressional relations office and State's business with "the Hill" was conducted in a haphazard but by no means always incompetent fashion. Now, however, there is an Assistant Secretary of State for Congressional Relations, who works full time on the problem. He is assisted by an impressive array of expediters, fact-finders, trip-arrangers, and escort officers, plus the machinery of a great Foreign Office. All of this is at the service of Congress. For every issue that becomes a matter of public debate or discord, there are scores that are quietly considered, arranged, acted upon and disposed of, alike to the satisfaction of the legislature and of the Chief Executive.

Certainly Congress could be less exigent in the matter of testimony, especially multiplicity and duplication of testimony by the Secretary of State and his principal subordinates. Certainly there could be a greater Congressional appreciation of the burdens created by their demands, not only for testimony, but for a wide assortment of other goods, services, and satisfactions, some of them whimsical in the extreme.

Certainly there should be a wider recognition of the value of professionalism in foreign affairs, just as the Congress has recognized the value of professional staffing on its own committees. If today's highly competitive entry into the nation's diplomatic service produces an aristocracy of brains and talent, then so much the better for the conduct of foreign affairs, and so much the worse for our enemies!

Certainly the American Foreign Service should not be

kept indefinitely on a starvation diet. For the cost of putting one astronaut in orbit, one hundred Ambassadors could do a more effective job of representing the American Government and the American people in that many foreign countries.[8]

Fundamentally, the problem of the relations between the Congress and the Executive over foreign policy is one established by the Constitution itself, inherent in the uneven distribution of power. Bipartisanship could perhaps be extended to cover a larger foreign affairs area, although under the two-party American system, where it is the responsibility of the opposition party to oppose, there are more practical limitations than some of the ardent proponents admit; in any case, bipartisanship has already contributed much to the strength of the foreign relations apparatus.

Short of the termination of the Cold War in a free world victory—short of the dawn of a new era of international serenity and good feeling (no date for which has yet been announced by the White House, the Kremlin, or Peking) the hauling and pulling of Congress and the Chief Executive over foreign affairs is likely to continue, while the inter-

---

[8] While diplomatic allowances in several particulars have improved, the worldwide figure for *representation* is still under one million dollars per annum—for the entire State Department service abroad—notwithstanding the fact that in ten years the number of Embassies to be supported has approximately doubled. This means that Ambassadors at many posts are still personally out of pocket because of their inescapable official representational responsibilities, and also that scarcely more than token funds can trickle down to their subordinates, many of whom after ten years of service can be allocated only a maximum of $250 a year. Members of the Embassy from other agencies of the Government—Treasury, Agriculture, Commerce, the military, et cetera, have much larger allowances than Foreign Service Officers of the same seniority, although the Foreign Service Officers have greater responsibilities.

CHAPTER 4

Tools of the Presidency: The Secretary of State and the Department of State

IF THE PRESIDENT CHOOSES TO WRAP HIMSELF IN A RED-white-and-blue cummerbund and caper in the White House rose garden with the Begum of Bugwallow, declaring that he does so in the name of foreign affairs, the Constitution of the United States (although not necessarily the electorate) will support his right to do so. If another President should elect to fill the White House with riffraff from the correspondence schools of *Academia,* and encourage them in the name of international relations to heckle the Secretary of State, again the Constitution would sustain the President. And if the next President should order the White House police, "Clear me out this nest of mummers," and return the conduct of international matters to the State Department, once more the Constitution could be cited to support an overdue housecleaning.

A President cannot, however, have it both ways. If he dances with the Begum while the academicians blow their woodwinds and call the tunes, his State Department will soon be reduced in stature and his Foreign Service will be relegated to counting American citizens insulted abroad and performing notarial services for visiting Senators. If a President, that is to say, is to have a strong and capable foreign affairs establishment—a Secretary and a Department of State and a Foreign Service worthy of their traditional responsibilities—he must clothe his Secretary of State with the prestige and authority of the Presidency itself. The Secretary must be "an extension of the President's responsibility," and unless he has the full confidence of the Chief Executive, he cannot function effectively.

The most comprehensive statement about the President and his foreign minister was made by a distinguished survivor of the latter office. Dean Acheson said the relationship between the two "will not prosper if the Secretary is not accepted as the President's principal adviser and executive agent in foreign affairs, and the trusted confidant of all his thoughts and plans relating to them."

"Principal adviser, executive agent and trusted confidant" probably sums up as well as it can be done the partnership between the Chief of State and his ranking cabinet aide, whose role was outlined in the legislation of 1789 establishing the office. That provides that the Secretary of State "shall perform ... such duties as shall ... be entrusted to him by the President of the United States" and that he shall conduct the business of the State Department "in such manner as the President ... shall from time to time order or instruct." [1]

It is thus a flexible and highly personal relationship, and the most successful examples of teamwork have been those in which the Secretary of State, albeit the junior partner,

---

[1] From *The Secretary of State*, a publication of the American Assembly of Columbia University, edited by Don K. Price, Prentice-Hall, Inc., Englewood Cliffs, N.J., 1960.

Dean Acheson, one of the contributors, was himself Secretary of State from 1949 to 1953, after a decade of apprenticeship as Assistant Secretary and then Under Secretary. Under two Presidents and four predecessor Secretaries, Mr. Acheson had an unparalleled opportunity to observe the machinery of foreign affairs in action.

has in fact shared the President's thoughts and plans and aspirations relating to international problems. In this century one thinks of John Hay, and two decades later of Charles Evans Hughes (whose President, however, had few thoughts), and more recently of Stimson, Marshall, Acheson, and Dulles. On the other hand, Secretaries of State who were bypassed by the President—Bryan and Lansing by Wilson, and Hull and Stettinius by Franklin Roosevelt —were handicapped in their operations, and the efficiency of the State Department suffered.[2]

Point one, therefore, is that the effectiveness of a Secretary of State depends on his closeness to the President and on the President's clear and constant support of his foreign minister. It follows that the President must delegate great authority to his Secretary of State, and that *in foreign affairs* the latter must have primacy over other interested agencies of the Government.

The second point is the existence of a series of factors which render vastly more complex than it should be the task of the senior member of the President's Cabinet. Here are some of them:

Executive appointees, including heads of Departments, are responsible not only to the President, but also to the Congress. That is the principle of "executive accountability and Congressional review"—the surveillance referred to in the preceding chapter. Congress rarely lets a Secretary of State forget it. But since Biblical times, serving two masters has corroded the body and spirit of the servant.

---

[2] Leaving present company aside, one can scarcely imagine a strong Secretary of State putting up with the kind of hatch-cover navigation that culminated in the hornpipe memoirs of recent participants. A strong captain would have lowered the boom on those midshipmen before the ship of state left port.

Again, foreign relations deal with environments outside the national domain, where the American capacity to control events is limited. This is not only true with respect to our adversaries, but almost equally true about our principal allies, as well—not to forget various small states posturing in our vicinity.[3]

Once again, the boundary between foreign and domestic policy is fuzzy and often difficult to trace. American internal decisions on such commodities as sugar and coffee, where the national interest is not always an altruistic interest, can literally enrich or bankrupt the foreign growers of those products. The same goes for copper and petroleum and many other products that enter into American consumption. Domestic food can also be a political weapon abroad.[4]

This smudged frontier between domestic questions and their effects abroad has led to a further complication. Bureaucrats from federal agencies other than the State

---

[3] Offensive Behavior as an Instrument of Foreign Policy is a notion dreamed up by the Communists—witness the conduct of Soviet delegates at countless international conferences. Witness also the "spontaneous demonstrations" organized to wreck this or deface that, or to destroy an American propaganda headquarters. Small states, noting the absence of penalties, adopted bad behavior with glee: Panama, Egypt, Cuba, and Haiti, for examples. To date, the United States has been unable to devise a way of making bad behavior expensive for the bad behaviorist. It may be some satisfaction to observe that dissident Communists are now sticking out their tongues and making provocative gestures toward their erstwhile mentor.

[4] The famous Food for Peace program about which Washington has uttered so many self-serving platitudes is an example of the effect of American agricultural policy on our foreign policy. To the world at large, including the beneficiaries, it still looks suspiciously like dumping, an interpretation not banished by recent Congressional debate about adding tobacco and alcoholic beverages to the list of "farm commodities" subsidized for the benefit of the American producers. Eventually, the Food for Peace advocates will probably vanish behind the smoke of the population explosion.

Department are encouraged to hang a red light over the doorway of diplomacy and then to crowd into the premises, where they abuse the piano player and call for drinks on the house. Once into foreign affairs, they act as though every night was Saturday night, and every day was Sunday.

And this is where there comes into play what an eminent public servant has called the "foul-up factor" in the administration and execution of Government policy. After viewing both the State and Defense Departments from within, Robert Lovett thus described the urge of the bureaucrat to meddle in the business of others:

"Just because some decision may affect his activities," said Secretary Lovett, "he thinks he automatically has a right to take part in making it."

Persistent assertion of this doctrine has blocked progress down half of the avenues in the District of Columbia, and nowhere with more adverse effect than in the State Department precinct.

To harass still further the existence of the Secretary of State, he must conduct his activities under an eye-searing glare of publicity. Gone are the days when the implementation of foreign policy could take place in private, and when what could not be settled today could be laid aside, to be coped with tomorrow, or a week or a month hence, whenever the climate might seem more propitious. Without publicity, national feelings could remain unruffled during the further search for an answer.

Today, however, foreign affairs are the province of everyone. The strivings of the President and the Secretary of State could scarcely be more revealed if they took place in a glass-windowed marineland, with porpoises acting like statesmen. The press conference has been turned into a televised circus, while the press itself glories in extracting the superfluous declaration. No meeting of American offi-

cials with foreign visitors is complete without a Joint Com-
muniqué, a prose form that has become as convincing as
the prefabricated deathbed confession.

Publicity and its accompanying lack of privacy are facts
of 20th-century life, along with instantaneous communication. But no single thing has more affected foreign relations
than fishbowl diplomacy.

If he survives all these hazards, the hard-pressed Secretary
of State must also be the adviser and executive agent of the
President, the operating head of a vast Government bureaucracy and its overseas personnel in the Foreign Service,
the formulator of new policies for Presidential consideration, and the negotiator of principal issues as well as the
explainer of those issues to the public and the defender
thereof before Congress. Finally, while playing the piano
himself, he must be the peacemaker among all those who
are striving to shoot the piano player.

So much for the Secretary of State, an official heavily
mortgaged by innumerable servitudes. The remarkable
thing is that candidates can still be found who seem willing,
even eager, to occupy the office.[5]

In the attempted fulfillment of his responsibilities, the
tools of the Secretary of State are the Department of State
in Washington and the American Foreign Service abroad.
They are the instruments by which international relations—
the day-to-day business arising among over one hundred

---

[5] Further calculation of the dimensions of the tasks facing the
Secretary of State are contained in the Jackson Subcommittee
Papers on the conduct of foreign policy, especially a volume entitled
The Secretary of State and the Ambassador (New York: Praeger,
1964). In addition to testimony from officers with long and varied
operational experience in foreign affairs, there is a stimulating
chapter by Professor Neustadt, at times consultant to the White
House, the State and Defense Departments, and the Bureau of the
Budget.

countries—are conducted. As the President must delegate authority to his associates, so the Secretary of State must in turn convey authority to his own subordinates, holding them accountable for the discharge of their duties.

In the last forty years the State Department has expanded tenfold—from seven hundred employees who used to pose with the Secretary of State for an annual photograph on the south steps of the old State War Navy Building—to over seven thousand, who now pose for identity cards without which they cannot enter the tabernacle of Foggy Bottom.

The officer corps of the Foreign Service has grown in the same period fourfold—from six hundred twenty-five to three thousand seven hundred, plus a Reserve of over one thousand, and Staff Corps personnel numbering about four thousand.[6]

The core of the State Department is its senior echelon, a handful of officers headed by the Under Secretary of State, and its five operational bureaus. They are known as the geographic Bureaus and they are: the European, which includes Canada and Soviet Russia; the Far Eastern, which excludes Ceylon, India, and points west; the Near Eastern and South Asian, which includes Greece and once included

---

[6] According to a recent State Department tabulation, of the 33,047 Americans serving in 1965 in our diplomatic missions abroad, only 7,295, or 22% were State Department employees, over one third of whom were engaged in providing "administrative support" for the other agencies represented—the United States Information Agency (propaganda), 1,166 or 4%; the Agency for International Development (handouts), 3,807 or 11%; the Peace Corps, 7,901 or 24%; Defense, including Attachés, Military Advisory Groups, etc., 10,983 or 33%; and others (presumably Treasury, Agricultural and Minerals Attachés, spooks, et cetera), 1,895 or 6%. Our missions in addition employed approximately ten thousand foreign nationals—visa clerks, administrative personnel, chauffeurs, messengers, et cetera. (This is in contrast to Communist embassies, which employ almost no citizens of the host country.)

Liberia; [7] the African, formed ten years ago to cope with
Emerging Nations; and the Latin American, now heir to
the new Caribbean countries and Guyana, inaugurated in
1966—the first addition to the roster of South American
nations since Bolívar.

The five geographic Bureaus deal with substantive
matters, primarily but not exclusively political in nature.
Added together, those five cover the world. They *are* the
State Department. The rest is service, liaison, communications, security, administration, personnel, housekeeping,
culture, management, and records—icing on the diplomatic
cake, fuel in the diplomatic motor, or dust in the diplomatic
dustbin, as the case may be.

Each geographic Bureau is headed by an Assistant Secretary of State and by one or more Deputies. Each geographic
Assistant Secretary is *ex officio* Chairman of the Interdepartmental Regional Group for the area in question, and
hence he should be the arbiter of American policy in the
countries concerned—subject only to the authority of the
Senior Interdepartmental Group whose Chairman is the
Under Secretary of State, to the Secretary himself, and to
the President.

Each geographic Bureau is likewise segmented geograph-

---

[7] Thereby hangs a tale. The Near Eastern officials, already having
jurisdiction over Egypt, coveted Algeria and Morocco, on the ground
that those areas are Moslem, too. The European Division, then as
now staffed with sagacious and wily young men, had acquired
Liberia years before, along with the African dependencies of European powers; the European Division was not averse to conceding
North Africa to the Near Easterners, but they ardently desired to
unload Liberia, as well. Citing the presence in Monrovia of Syrian
and Lebanese traders and arguing that those were proper wards of
the Near Eastern Division, a package deal was negotiated—Algeria
and Morocco plus Liberia—and the Near East was stuck with
Liberia for nearly twenty years thereafter—until the African Bureau
was founded in the late 1950s.

ically—e.g., the Office of Greek, Turkish, and Iranian Affairs in the Bureau of Near East and South Asian Affairs; or the Office of Central American Affairs—dealing with Costa Rica, Nicaragua, Honduras, Salvador, and Guatemala—in the Bureau of Latin American Affairs.

The low man on the geographic totem pole was until recently called a Country Desk Officer (now Country Director), and a very important individual he is and always has been, since he receives the "action copies" of messages from the American Embassy in his country, and he is responsible for what happens next. It is the Country Director who drafts the substantive outgoing messages—"instructions," as they are known to the trade—clears them with his immediate superiors, and gets them on the wire to the waiting American Ambassador abroad.

The Country Director seeks to do all that is useful and needful on behalf of the American Embassy in "his" country, and so key an official is he that the first thing a newly appointed Ambassador should do is to ascertain the identity and competence of the official occupying the home office desk, since much of ambassadorial performance will depend on the quality of the Potomac backstopping he receives from his Country Director.

The Country Director is also the primary liaison official between the State Department and the Washington Embassy of the country of his responsibility. Wise foreign Ambassadors will transact from seventy-five to ninety percent of their business not with the Secretary of State or with the corresponding geographic Assistant Secretary, but with the "man on the desk who knows the answers," a mature officer with a dozen or more years of service, including service in the Ambassador's country, who speaks the language of that country and is familiar with its customs, institutions, and problems.

The most competent Foreign Service Officers have traditionally been selected for assignment to the geographic
Bureaus of the State Department, and successful performance there often marks an officer as "Chief of Mission
material." Conversely, if an officer proves ineffectual in
handling a country desk, the chances are that his career
may end in the doldrums of administration or housekeeping, or if he speaks French, as Consul in some African
outpost.

An experiment is currently going on, seeking to upgrade
the country desk officer—calling him Country Director is a
manifestation of it—by appointing former Ambassadors
to those departmental positions. Proponents believe that
this would add consequence to the position and be consonant with the increased responsibility of the State Department under the President's directive of March 1966—
NSAM-341, described in Chapter 2. This proposal in effect
would erect longer and taller totem poles: the Country
Director (former Ambassador or not) would still be the
low man on the pole, although he might now be farther off
the ground than before. As a practical proposition, filling
the Department with unfrocked Ambassadors and encouraging them to drum like cock partridges on Foggy
Bottom logs might shortly deafen the rest of the State
Department. A few of the most important country desks—
those corresponding to the old list of Class One posts
abroad—might perhaps rate ambassadorial rank, but the
majority would be better served by officers of lower grade
and fewer pretensions.[8]

----

[8] Officers of Classes Four, Three, and Two, from which the majority of Country Directors should continue to come, will have had
from ten to twenty years of service overseas.

Until World War II, a Country Desk Officer often had more
than one country, and in some cases he had several. In the European
Division in the 1930s, for example, the affairs of the three Scandi-

To see how a Country Director operates, let us examine a not-so-mythical case, illustrative of the handling of a foreign affairs problem in the Department of State.

A segment in Central America of the Inter-American Highway needs repair. A request for assistance is made by the Guataraguan Government. Guataragua urges, moreover, that the entire segment be relocated, allegedly to avoid some foothills inland from the coast, and that financing of this construction be undertaken by the American Government under the program of *Alianza para el Progreso*.

The corresponding Guataraguan Note, formalizing this request, is handed to the Country Director by the Guataraguan Ambassador in Washington—who addresses the Country Director as *"viejo amigo"* and *"querido colega"* and sometimes as *"tu."* Attached to the Note are engineering studies, a finding by the Bureau of Public Roads prepared at the instance of the Guataraguan Government, and a price tag of twenty-five million dollars.

A simple and straightforward proposal, declares the Guataraguan Ambassador. He will be grateful if his *viejo amigo* will kindly expedite action; a favorable reply will be gratifying likewise to His Excellency the President of the Republic, whose dedication to public works is equaled only by his enthusiasm for *Alianza para el Progreso*.

---

navian countries, plus those of Holland, Portugal, and Spain—six countries altogether—were assigned to a single officer, who in his spare time played tennis at Chevy Chase and swam in the Potomac.

The equivalent officer today is multiplied by half a dozen, and there is already a movement to give the newly designated Country Director something bigger to direct than a desk and the view from his totem pole: clearly we shall soon be seeing Deputy Country Directors and Assistant Country Directors, plus Executive Assistants and Special Assistants and Administrative Assistants to the Country Director—all the paraphernalia of Parkinson's Law in happy conjunction. And these officials will keep one another so busy that none of them will have time for tennis or swimming.

Within the next few days, the Guataraguan project involves no less than *fourteen* different agencies of the American Government. The Bureau of Public Roads, whose emissary has just returned from Tegucifagasta, is enthusiastic about the proposed construction; however, the Bureau is fresh out of money. The Export Import Bank might lend the required funds, but the Guataraguan Ambassador has intimated to his *querido colega* that Guataragua would prefer a so-called soft loan, with no interest during a grace period of twelve years, and payment thereafter in counterpart *pesos*, generated by a Food for Peace transaction.[9]

This puts the Agency for International Development into the picture, along with the Inter-American Development Bank, established to extend soft loans. Anticipating events, the Treasury Department names a representative.

These are all officials legitimately interested in the Guataraguan highway proposal. There are presently peripheral participants, who are no less articulate. The Department of Agriculture is alerted because *sigatoka*, a disease of the banana, is prevalent around Puerto Toronja, the principal town on the new route, where an American fruit company has interests. A *sigatoka* expert is mobilized. Ditto the Public Health Service, which through the Pan American Sanitary Bureau and the World Health Organization is eager to campaign for the eradication of *paludismo*—in English, malaria.

The Bureau of Mines is quickly followed by the Department of Justice and the Federal Bureau of Investigation—the first because the proposed route passes an old Spanish gold mine, which has recently been reactivated by an American citizen; and Justice and the F.B.I. because the same American citizen is wanted in an embezzlement case—

---

[9] A euphemism for saying that the highway would be constructed at the expense of the American taxpayers.

a matter of frustration because Guataragua has no extradition treaty with the United States.

Next comes the Peace Corps, which has announced the acquisition of a portable latrine that can be carried in a handbag and pops open like an umbrella; just the thing for highway construction workers, who will soon be in need of temporary housing (and plumbing). The Peace Corps also offers to establish a Project, complete with Volunteers, to teach basket weaving to the camp followers of the bulldozer operators. *Jipijapa* fiber, which in Ecuador makes Panama hats, is reported to grow wild on the coast of Guataragua.

Finally comes the Commerce Department, which is eager to sell something abroad, road machinery, maybe, to help stem the drain on the dollar.

Thirteen American officials, not counting the Country Director for Guataragua in the State Department, are now considering the desirability of constructing a highway in Central America. Three of them—the *sigatoka* expert, the Bureau of Public Roads man, and the Country Director— have served in Guataragua, and most of the rest of them could find it on a map. All are busy studying their lessons and preparing Position Papers for their respective agencies and departments.

The Guataraguan Ambassador presently becomes impatient. He declares that with the advent of the rainy season, the existing highway will soon become difficult to transit, if not impassable. After telephoning to the Country Director, whom he this time addresses as *Señor Director*, he seeks an interview with the Secretary of State, to whom he complains about the delay, which the Ambassador implies is inconsistent with the Spirit of Punta del Este.[10]

---

[10] Where a conference took place in 1961, at which the United States was hotly importuned to liberalize the rules governing Ameri-

The Ambassador adds that if ever the Panama Canal should be destroyed, the United States could always count on friendly Guataragua to facilitate the passage of American forces across the Guataraguan portion of the Inter-American Highway.

The Secretary of State, slightly bewildered, passes this on to the Assistant Secretary of State for Latin American Affairs. That official summons the Country Director, who in the meantime has carefully assembled what the late General Marshall, a precisionist in matters of staff, used to term the Facts Bearing on the Problem.

The facts bearing on the Guataraguan highway project include the following:

(a) The existing highway is in fact in need of repairs. They should have been undertaken several years ago, when a recommendation to that effect was first made by the Bureau of Public Roads. Guataraguan representations to the contrary, however, the road is not in imminent danger of becoming impassable.

(b) Repairs to the existing highway would probably cost between three and four million dollars, including reconditioning the American roadbuilding equipment already on hand.

(c) The proposed new highway would be thirteen kilometers (about eight miles) longer than the segment it is intended to replace. There are no towns of importance on the new route except Puerto Toronja, which is adequately served by sea, and no industrial development except *Minas del Toro Manso*, the gold mine reactivated by the alleged fugitive from justice—who has not been heard from.

----

can financing of *Alianza para el Progreso* projects. When the United States agreed, the complaints were temporarily muted; this became known as the Spirit of Punta del Este (Uruguay). The same theme was reiterated at a second meeting at Punta del Este in 1967.

(d) The alternate route is closer to the coast than the existing one; much of the terrain is marshy, and there are numerous small rivers, swollen in the rainy season; they would have to be bridged. Cost estimates must accordingly be viewed with reserve. The Public Roads estimate is twenty-five million dollars, but the Bureau admits that actual costs could be "considerably higher."

(e) Guataragua is now enjoying a period of prosperity, with favorable prices for coffee, cacao, and bananas. Its finances are in the best shape in a decade.

These findings having been checked with the American Ambassador in Tegucifagasta, the Ambassador concurs in the following recommendations:

(1) That Guataragua be urged to repair the existing highway, for which purpose *Alianza para el Progreso* financing can readily be made available; and

(2) That Guataragua be informed that if it desires to go forward with the construction of the costly alternate route, commercial financing be sought, in default of which an Export Import Bank dollar loan might be arranged, on approximately the same terms.

The Country Director appends a draft note to the foregoing effect prepared for signature by the Secretary of State, in reply to the Note from the Guataraguan Ambassador.

In the era before the (1966) White House directive giving the State Department authority in questions of foreign affairs that involve other agencies, Secretary Lovett's "foul-up factor" would long since have been in operation, and the Guataraguan Ambassador might have had better grounds to complain about the delay. As it is, the Bureau of Public Roads heads the clamor for approval of the new route. The Bureau is supported by the Agency for International Development, which has an aggressive representative in Guataragua, eager to find *Alianza para el Progreso* projects in which to invest, and large funds at his disposal; and by the Inter-American Development Bank, likewise with funds, whose Directors are still smarting from charges aired by the Good Neighbors at the last ECLA ECOSOC [11] Conference that the United States is shirking its responsibilities toward Latin American economic collaboration.

The Peace Corps, like the Agency for International Development, has been trying for some time to establish a beachhead in Guataragua; it perceives little romance in reconditioned roadbuilding machinery. The Corps assumes what it describes as a Forward-Looking Posture. Agriculture, busy installing a *sigatoka* research center at Puerto Toronja, thinks the new highway might be "helpful." The Public Health Service does, too, on the grounds that the influx of construction workers and Peace Corps Volunteers might lead to greater public awareness of the importance of continuing the campaign against malaria.

Commerce and the Bureau of Mines, with their eyes by now on other sparrows, express no opinion. Treasury goes along with State. Justice and the F.B.I. will be satisfied if the Embassy in Tegucifagasta continues to keep tabs on the owner of *Minas del Toro Manso* (Mines of the Gentle Bull), which is reportedly making pots of money.

None of these officials is unpatriotic, and not all of them are self-seeking. They are merely ambitious for their respective agencies to be up and doing the kinds of things they think they were created by Congress to do: building roads, promoting public (and agricultural) health, lending money, and encouraging the natives to Learn a Handicraft, in order to lessen the dependence of the economy on world commodities with fluctuating prices.

They call these activities Waging Peace; an opponent of

---

[11] Economic Commission for Latin America of the Economic and Social Council of United Nations.

Waging Peace is a Reactionary, out of step with the New Diplomacy.

The fact that the personnel of most of these agencies have had limited experience abroad diminishes no whit their enthusiasm for making available to Emerging Nations the fruits of American technology, enriched by the vitamins of American culture, and subsidized by the American dollar.

Give them a Project. They will christen it Pegasus and be off through the bright blue yonder.

In these exhilarating circumstances, the role of the State Department sometimes seems to them to be that of the spoilsport, who not only lacks the zeal of the crusader for the revolution of rising expectations, but who at the mention of Pegasus has been known to reach for a lariat or even a rifle.[12]

---

[12] Even with the foul-up factor removed, Guataragua soon obtained both roads. The repair job was promptly undertaken and completed for less than the estimated four million dollars, but that evoked little satisfaction on the part of a disgruntled Guataraguan Government. Pouting, Guataragua thereupon put on an act the keynotes of which were that the United States was insincere in its declared attachment to the ideals of inter-American cooperation, and that the Spirit of Punta del Este had been forgotten. This performance went on for some time, before appreciative audiences at United Nations and at several Pan American Conferences, during which the State Department's position was eroded by the activities of the Washington agencies interested in building the new highway and by the departure of the Country Director, who, having completed his tour of duty in the State Department, was assigned to Spain.

The final cost of building the new highway via Puerto Toronja was sixty-three million dollars, and the Department of Agriculture spent additional funds on the *sigatoka* research laboratory.

The American owner of *Minas del Toro Manso* became a naturalized citizen of Guataragua. To celebrate, he gave ten thousand dollars to the favorite charity of the wife of the President of the Republic—a foundling home called the Immaculate Conception.

The Peace Corps prudently switched from basket weaving to birth control, but then ran afoul of the Bishop of Tegucifagasta. Most of the Volunteers escaped malaria.

In the Department of State, at any given moment, several score Country Directors will be working on countless plans, projects, altercations, agreements, disputes, and understandings, each more or less complicated than a highway problem in Central America, and each focusing the attention of swarms of busy officials. Not all of them cost the taxpayers money, and many of them are quite expeditiously settled, if not by the Country Director himself, then upon intermediate or higher levels, up to the Secretary of State or even the President.

Nor should it be inferred that Country Directors spend the bulk of their time on inconsequential matters. They are likewise the officials who, by reference from above, work on the Cold War, the hot war, the pandemonium in Africa, the growing pains of NATO (which was born in the Bureau of European Affairs), and all the other problems besetting a troubled world under the constant pressure of change. Large problems and small ones, in sum they form the mosaic, made of literally thousands of cases a year, called the foreign relations of the United States.

Although the five geographic Bureaus, together with the small echelon of senior officials, bear the brunt of the substantive work of the State Department, there are other offices of importance, cutting across geographic lines. The Bureau of Economic Affairs is one; it probably reached its greatest influence during the long Cordell Hull regime. The domain of the Legal Adviser is another; he is the Secretary's principal assistant in matters of international law. (Most Secretaries of State have themselves been lawyers.) A third is the Congressional Relations Bureau, already mentioned.

One of the most interesting corners of the State Department is occupied by the Policy Planning Staff, established twenty years ago by Dean Acheson, with George Kennan as its first Chairman. It got off to a slow start because its first personnel, including some of the most talented Foreign Service Officers in the corps, were in such continuing demand for brushfire operations, to the detriment of their long-range projections. (The National Security Council faces the same problem.)

By now the Policy Planning Staff has settled down, and although forward planning in foreign affairs has its limitations (including the infinity of variants which prevent things from happening in the way plotted beforehand by the planners), nevertheless an idea factory in a foreign ministry possesses a powerful potential. If precise computations are impossible, planning can nevertheless include goals and objectives of foreign affairs, as well as the development of policies to attain them. Existing policies can be scrutinized for defects or obsolescence, or—like "no entangling alliances"—for relevancy to changed conditions.

Lastly, a planning staff can be a happy and productive meeting ground for professors and theoreticians on the one hand, and for operating personnel on the other—each benefiting from the background and experience of the other.

Here are sample questions for the policy planners:

1. Take the "future of Cuba." What should the United States do when Communism is overthrown and the Cuban people regain their freedom? More specifically, what should happen to the private property of American citizens, first looted and then nationalized by Castro? Should the American Government be prepared to assert the right of its dispossessed citizens to resume immediate control of their properties—worth at the time of the collapse of the Batista Government more than two and a half billion dollars—or should the official emphasis be on assisting the Cuban people to set up a new administration, one of whose several tasks would be the sorting out of expropriated property,

Cuban as well as foreign, and the equitable disposition of it?

2. Again—what should be the attitude of the American Government toward certain areas of Africa when it becomes apparent, even to the most fervent United States desegregationists, that independence is not the solution? Or when, later still, the American people are forced to conclude not only that there may be no *satisfactory* solution, but perhaps *no* solution whatever?

3. Or, simply, what do we do if we don't win, in Vietnam?

At the top of the State Department totem pole is an upper echelon that includes the Under Secretary, an Under Secretary for Economic Affairs, and a Deputy Under Secretary for Political Affairs, who has recently been the ranking Foreign Service Officer in the Department.[13] There are roving Special Ambassadors—for example, one to advise the President on Soviet Affairs, and another to calibrate Vietnam peace activities—and there are hordes of Assistant and Deputy Assistant Secretaries, including the senior ones who head the geographic Bureaus.

Lastly, there is a Deputy Under Secretary of State for Administration, during whose tenures since 1962 the State Department has become possibly the most over-administered agency in the District of Columbia. Since an account

---

[13] Freeman Matthews, Robert Murphy, Livingston Merchant, Alexis Johnson, Foy Kohler, and Charles Bohlen have been recent Deputy Under Secretaries for Political Affairs—each holding the topmost rank of Career Ambassador in the Foreign Service.

A suggestion is pending to add a Permanent Under Secretary of State to the roster, to rank after the Secretary and the Under Secretary. The purposes would be to assure continuity, especially during the confused period of changing administrations when the politically appointed hierarchy departs en masse, and to give the Foreign Service more adequate representation. This is discussed in Chapter 5.

of these depredations might be tedious for the non-specialist in Potomac necromancy, a chart is included in the Appendix, whereby a recent incumbent sought to render intelligible his operations.

The chart shows forty-seven different ways of confusing the issue. An office of Budget Planning and Presentation competes for attention with an office of Financial Management Systems Program. An office for Substantive Information Systems Program has two maladjusted dependents: the Organizational Studies and Procedures Program, and the Management Suggestions and Consultation Program. But the forty-seven varieties on display obscure fifty percent of the wares. Five additional major divisions, which possibly add up to another forty-seven programs and offices and panels and evaluations, are listed by titles only, including a Bureau of Security and Consular Affairs, and a separate Office of Security.[14]

In this gloomy edifice of bureaucratic splendor the stranger prowls about, bemused, and even the Secretary of State must occasionally wonder how convoluted management can get, before the entire crenelated contraption of glue, cardboard, and paper clips collapses around the ears of its architects, leaving a stain on the rug perhaps eradicable by insect repellent.

Fortunately for the diplomacy of the United States, diplomacy has shown sufficient stamina and has proved sufficiently durable so that not even the experts in adminis-

---

[14] This Chart was issued by a Deputy Under Secretary of State for Administration in July 1966, along with an explanatory Circular announcing that "effective immediately," in the office of the Deputy Under Secretary of State for Administration, a special Executive Group was established, in order to administer the administrators. Simultaneously an Executive Secretariat was organized "to support the operations of the Executive Group" in administering the administrators. The text follows the chart.

tration have been able to wreck it, although they have seriously dented the operation of the Foreign Service, as described in the following chapter.

The old State Department system of geographic Bureaus and the movement of cases from the bottom toward the top, and from the Secretary of State to the Country Director, still works reasonably well. That system works remarkably well, granted the size of the Government establishment and the gigantic appropriations the Congress continues to approve for activities conducted by the American Government abroad—in contrast to nigggardly amounts appropriated to enable the State Department to police those activities. It even works notwithstanding the attraction of foreign affairs for those not versed in them and the mounting number of countries that are engaged either in weaving the fabric of international relations or in trying to destroy that fabric before the free nations can make a garment of it.

The system works, that is to observe, in spite of the administrators.

CHAPTER 5

Tools of the Presidency: The American Foreign Service ≋

THE AMERICAN FOREIGN SERVICE DATES FROM 1924, WHEN the then separate diplomatic and consular services were combined in a single organization, with promotion based on merit.[1] The amalgamation was more popular with the Coolidge Administration than it was with the diplomats, some of whom complained that consuls—limited in their experience to dealing with foreign mayors, prefects, chiefs of police, and captains of the port—lacked understanding of the broader international issues handled by diplomats with higher officials of the central government.

Furthermore, the diplomats, who at the time numbered about one hundred and twenty-five officers against five hundred consuls, enjoyed wider privileges and immunities than consular officials, and numerous diplomats apprehended that creating a combined service might eventually dilute their status and hence affect their prestige. (Twenty-five years later that in fact occurred, but for different reasons; by that time, everybody was playing diplomacy).[2]

---

[1] This was the Rogers Act, dated May 24, 1924, named for Representative John Jacob Rogers of Massachusetts.

[2] Notwithstanding the attitude of certain 1924 diplomats, their separate service, so inadequately paid that no one lacking private

62

Secretary of State Charles Evans Hughes was enthusiastic about the Foreign Service he had helped to create. He declared that "the new diplomacy is an old art practiced under new conditions.... The new diplomacy deals formally with governments but actually with peoples that control governments.... Increase in the facilities of communication makes personal contacts even more necessary. No mechanism will ever take the place of interviews of men who respect and trust each other.... Democracy with its new diplomacy should be served expertly, and the faithful Foreign Service Officer should have the inspiration and the satisfaction of the assurance that the nature and importance of his service are appreciated at home...." [3]

Thus auspiciously launched, with an improved salary scale and with provision for allowances and reimbursements that Congress has gradually implemented across the years, the Foreign Service from its beginning has attracted high-caliber candidates from all over the country. This enthusi-

---

resources could accept appointment in it, contained a remarkably high proportion of talented and dedicated public servants. The names stand out of such men as William Phillips, Henry White, Joseph Grew, Henry Fletcher, Jefferson Caffery (whose thirty years as Ambassador remain a record), Norman Armour, and Hugh Gibson; and among the younger officers serving forty years ago, of Theodore Marriner, Pierrepont Moffat, Allen Dulles, Ray Atherton, Alexander Kirk, Herschel Johnson, and Freeman Matthews.

The old consular service was more modestly manned. Nevertheless, a number of former consuls became Ambassadors in the decades that followed the Rogers Act, among them Robert Murphy and Loy Henderson, two of the most prominent American diplomats of the post-World War II years.

[3] *The Foreign Service of the United States* by Tracy H. Lay, a former consular officer. (New York: Prentice-Hall, 1925.) The quotations are from the Foreword by Secretary Hughes, whose reiterated references to the "new diplomacy" of forty years ago should be of interest to those who after World War II sought to claim credit for originating the phrase.

asm on the part of superior young people persists to this day, notwithstanding the fact that of several thousand applicants who take the examinations each year, less than five percent are eventually commissioned, and for those accepted there is much routine between Vice Consul and Chief of Mission.

In over four decades since the Rogers Act, the number of countries with which the United States does business has multiplied threefold (to over one hundred and twenty), with additional nations, candidates at birth for American largesse, still hatching in the United Nations incubator.

Foreign Service Officers have proliferated at an even higher rate—from six hundred in 1924 to approaching four thousand today. This personnel expansion and resulting over-staffing of embassies accounts for one of the two principal things that are wrong with the Foreign Service (the other is administration). Ironically, over-staffing began with the *under*-staffing of World War II, when recruiting was suspended and President Roosevelt, no friend of professional diplomats, sometimes gave the impression that he thought those already holding Presidential commissions in the Foreign Service were evading the draft.

Almost as soon as hostilities ended, American Government projects started to burgeon abroad, and each project involved American personnel going overseas—hundreds and hundreds of American civilians replacing the demobilized World War II veterans who had returned to the United States. Most of these civilians had little experience in dealing with foreigners, and none at all in diplomacy.

No ark was ever more crowded than the postwar ship of state with these amateur argonauts, who presently sighting Cathay, swarmed ashore, whooping. What with the Marshall Plan to revitalize Western Europe, and the Truman Plan to rescue Greece and Turkey, and the Point Four Plan to share technical skills with the Alacalufas and the Igorots, and the aid programs to accelerate the revolution of rising expectations, and the U.S.I.A. plan to build the biggest megaphone that propaganda ever poured hot words through —those postwar years represented the heyday of the factotum with a mission, wreaking the American way of life on a weary world.

This was the New Diplomacy of the decade following Hiroshima. It was a blissful decade for those spending the taxpayers' money on saving the heathen, but it was a difficult time for the Foreign Service, with its roster at the end of the war still frozen at the pre-Pearl Harbor level.

Two steps were taken on behalf of the Foreign Service in 1946. The first was the Manpower Act, an emergency measure authorizing the entry at grades compatible with previous experience of an additional two hundred and fifty officers. Entrants were recruited mostly from the disbanding military, from various civilian wartime agencies, and from the Department of State.[4]

The second step was the Foreign Service Act of 1946, the first general legislation since the Rogers Act twenty-two years before. With various amendments, the 1946 Act governs the Foreign Service today. It provided a revised salary scale to take account of the inflation of World War II; the post of Director General of the Foreign Service was created; and the grades of Career Minister and (in 1955) Career Ambassador were established as the topmost rungs of the Foreign Service promotion ladder. In addition, a useful Foreign Service Reserve was established, more liberal

---

[4] The Manpower Act recruited first-rate people. They included Livingston Merchant, who retired in 1962 as Deputy Under Secretary of State for Political Affairs, and Thomas Mann, who retired in 1966 after serving as Assistant Secretary for Latin American Affairs, as Ambassador to Mexico, and as Under Secretary for Economic Affairs.

retirement benefits were provided, and the old Foreign Service School in the State Department was given a face-lifting and rechristened the Foreign Service Institute.

Pressure to enlarge the Foreign Service still further continued. The Manpower Act of 1946 was followed by a campaign for more lateral entry, but that project soon collided with a perfectionist heading the entry procedure, who believed that the standards of the Foreign Service were the highest in the world and ought not to be lowered. Few of the lateral entry applicants, including those from the Department of State itself, were able to surmount the qualifications hurdle erected by the chief examiner. The frustration of the rejected candidates emphasized an unfortunate cleavage between State Department personnel and Foreign Service Officers, whereas obviously a successful foreign affairs establishment demands the maximum of flexibility between the home service and service abroad.

There were other difficulties. Still vastly outnumbered abroad by the non-diplomats of agencies other than the State Department, it was inevitable that Foreign Service personnel, more sophisticated than the newcomers in dealing with citizens of other lands, would be skeptical of certain postwar operations, including the wisdom of monkeying with the political institutions of host countries, or the imminence of a millennium ushered in by American handouts. When Foreign Service Officers tangled with the proponents of aid, the diplomats were denounced as reactionaries, out of step with the modern procession. The demand swelled for replacement diplomats, attuned to the New Revelation.[5]

---

[5] The State Department, groping for definitions, later produced these pearls of wisdom: "*International Relations* covers relationships between sovereign states that form the core of traditional diplomacy—negotiations, bilateral agreements, trade, efforts to in-

7

6 6 6 6 6 6 6 6 6 6

It might be an exaggeration to say that the State Department, for several years after the war, was relegated to issuing passports for aid program directors, or that the Foreign Service spent that time operating motor pools for the practitioners of the New Diplomacy, but it would not stretch credulity to observe that greater chaos has rarely reigned overseas than it did among the civilian officials and employees of the American Government who during that time raced up and down the playing fields of foreign lands.

By the time the Eisenhower Administration had unpacked its suitcases in Washington, and John Foster Dulles had racked up his first hundred thousand miles of airplane travel, it began to dawn upon Potomac officials that something ought to be done. In due course, a committee was appointed to examine, to meditate, and to recommend.

This was the famous Wriston Committee, named for its Chairman, Dr. Henry M. Wriston, president of Brown University. Its findings were adopted, including the irrational notion that what were needed abroad were not fewer extraneous personnel, but more Foreign Service Indians.

---

fluence foreign policy, and so forth. *Internal Development* covers the operational programs that have sprung up since World War II by which the United States attempts to effect the development of the host society. In a highly developed industrial society most of the resources will show up in *International Relations* and little or nothing will show up in *Internal Development*. In a lesser developed country most of the resources will show up in *Internal Development* and little or nothing will show up in *International Relations*. . . . [This] has also proved to be a useful device for clarifying thinking about basic intent. For example, one must be clear about whether a given political activity is aimed at improving relationships between two countries or toward development of political institutions in the host country."

From a pamphlet entitled "The Comprehensive Country Programming System," a major effort on the part of the planners, unveiled in 1964. "Traditional diplomacy" is airily dismissed with "and so forth."

That was the equivalent of saying that the way to cure congestion is to add more people.

The Foreign Service was accordingly doubled—from fifteen hundred officers to over three thousand—primarily by the device of dragooning key personnel of the State Department and making Foreign Service Officers of them. It was a painful process, violating in many instances the terms of reference of those who had been employed for Potomac, not foreign, service, and who did not aspire to serve abroad. Middle-aged departmental officers with the Bethesda mortgage half paid off found themselves exiled to Paraguay with no knowledge of Guarani, or sent to serve as Consul General in Frankfort without ever before having set foot in a consulate.

Not only did many of the "wristonees" lack knowledge of Foreign Service laws, regulations, and procedure, but they lacked as well interest in or aptitude for careers abroad.

At the same time, their posts in the State Department were designated as "Foreign Service Officer positions" and manned by officers brought in from the field, whose inexperience in treading the tortuous paths of bureaucracy adversely affected home office operations.

Here also arose the problem of the generalist versus the specialist, and it proved so difficult to fill many of the positions in the State Department that by 1960, five years after the inception of the Wriston program, three hundred of approximately fifteen hundred departmental posts that had been designated "Foreign Service Officer positions," had to be "de-designated"—that is, changed back to being departmental positions.[6]

Another corrosive problem involved salaries. Entry into

---

[6] These were mostly in functional rather than geographical operations: intelligence and research, cultural and educational affairs, policy planning, "and so forth."

the State Department had generally been without formal examination, and once hired, the position governed the pay. In the Foreign Service, in contrast, the class to which the officer had been promoted—rather than the task he might at any given moment be performing—governed his salary. Since it was decided that the "wristonization" of State Department officers should not result in reduction in pay, numerous officers were blanketed into the Foreign Service at grades higher than if they had spent comparable years exposed to the highly competitive Foreign Service promotion system.

Still another result of the Wriston program was the wrecking of the Staff Corps, as presently described, by transferring its upper echelons into the Foreign Service.[7]

In the clairvoyance of that hindsight which seldom fails to cast a rosy glow of satisfaction upon second-guessers, it is now apparent that what was most needed at the time of the Wriston program a dozen years ago was not a massive enlargement of the Foreign Service, but a reestablishment of the authority of the Secretary of State over the conduct of foreign relations. Without the latter, every agency in

---

[7] Those interested in details of the integration program are referred to a volume of the American Assembly, already cited: *The Secretary of State*, Prentice-Hall, Inc., Englewood Cliffs, N.J., 1960. Chapter Four contains a spirited defense of the Wriston program, contributed by Dr. Wriston himself.

A contrary view, entitled "The Future of Our Diplomacy," was expressed by George F. Kennan, a Foreign Service Officer for a quarter-century before his resignation early in the Eisenhower Administration. Ambassador Kennan's observations on "wristonization" are contained in an article published in *Foreign Affairs* in July 1955 (Volume 33, No. 41).

Another source, full of bureaucratic prose but packed with facts and figures, is a pamphlet published in 1960 by the Foreign Relations Committee of the Senate. It is entitled "Administration of the Department of State," Government Printing Office, August 26, 1960.

Washington with activities and personnel abroad—which at that time meant practically every agency in Washington —continued to be its own judge of the importance and the urgency of its projects. And once these agents were abroad, there was no way to regiment them, far less to control them or to establish priorities, or even to keep their eager beavers from felling the cherished poplar trees that lined so many foreign highways.[8]

In one important particular, however, the Wriston program was highly successful. By integrating State Department personnel with Foreign Service personnel, a degree of administrative flexibility was finally achieved. That was a major gain. The hands of the Secretary of State had hitherto been tied, and he had been handicapped in coping with personnel problems, at great cost to the efficiency of operations.

Moreover, many of the pains engendered by the forcible aspects of the program have now worn off. The worst integration misfits have been weeded out, or retired, and the successful "wristonees" have been promoted step by step with their Foreign Service colleagues. As was the case after the amalgamation of the diplomatic and consular services

---

[8] An Eisenhower edict was issued in 1956, declaring that the American Ambassador was the ranking United States official abroad. That was comforting news to Ambassadors, except that no corresponding authority was vested in them. Ambassadors could march at the head of their overstuffed staffs on ceremonial occasions, but Ambassadors were not authorized to hire or fire the personnel of other agencies, or to direct their local operations, or to interfere with the correspondence sent to their respective home offices in Washington, with the result that those offices kept on receiving reports at variance with those reaching the State Department over the Ambassador's signature.

It was not until President Johnson's directive of 1966, described in Chapter 2, that the necessary State Department authority was belatedly forthcoming.

in 1924, the origins of individual officers soon ceased to be meaningful: it was their performance as Foreign Service Officers that counted.

How good then is the American Foreign Service today, and what are its prospects?

A fair answer would be that the Foreign Service is better than the press and the Congress sometimes profess to believe, but still not as good as it ought to be. And its deficiencies are primarily the fault of the parent organization, the Department of State.[9]

---

[9] An indication of the kind of young people who are interested in the Foreign Service as a career is contained in the questions they ask about it. The three principal questions in the minds of potential candidates are:

First, can I live on my government salary? The answer is, Yes, you can—unless you are appointed Ambassador to one of the more expensive capitals, in which case private resources are still essential.

Secondly, to what extent are politics involved in Foreign Service promotions? The answer is that politics have no bearing whatever either on selection for a Foreign Service commission in the first place, or on promotion through the eight grades to Career Minister and Career Ambassador. That is one of the strengths of the Foreign Service, contributing greatly to esprit de corps.

However, when it comes to appointment as Ambassador, after an officer through competition and the merit system has reached the upper ranks of the career service, it should be remembered that one man in three is still appointed from outside the Foreign Service. Furthermore, the ratio is more unfavorable to professionals than one-out-of-three implies, since political appointees often get the "good" posts, whereas it is seldom that La Paz, Ouagadougou, or Reykjavik is not occupied by an Ambassador from the career. That is one of the weaknesses of the Foreign Service, impairing its esprit de corps.

Thirdly, once commissioned by the President, am I likely to get interesting or challenging work as a junior Foreign Service Officer? The answer to that is a qualified affirmative. It used to be that the Foreign Service provided challenging work for everyone, juniors and seniors alike. It still does, in some places, but the situation has been eroded by the current overstaffing of many posts and by over-

Few Secretaries since Hughes (1921 to 1925) have taken a personal interest in either the mechanics or the morale of the Foreign Service. Buried under substantive issues and accumulated chores, Secretaries have left administration to deputies and have paid scant attention to running the Department of State. Even Dean Acheson (1948 to 1953), while respecting and utilizing many talented individuals in the Foreign Service, devoted little time to the organization as such. And John Foster Dulles (1953 to 1959), entering upon his duties with a more intimate knowledge of the organization than most holders of the office, nevertheless, permitted Senator McCarthy practically to tear it to pieces in 1953.[10]

The Foreign Service entered the decade of the 1960s with far too many people. The notion that it takes scores of officials to man a single Embassy, and thousands and thousands to operate a successful Washington foreign affairs establishment, has proved in post after post and country

---

administration emanating from the State Department itself. Neither should be vital to a career in the Foreign Service, but at present it admittedly affects it.

[10] The viciousness of the McCarthy period had to be experienced to be believed: wild, unsupported charges about "card-carrying Communists" within the State Department itself, and an equally poisonous campaign against so-called personal security risks. It was during this time that the author, then serving as Ambassador, inherited a loyal and capable bachelor deputy. The deputy became eligible for home leave at the height of the McCarthy depredations, and he remarked on his departure for the United States that he had better find himself a wife forthwith "because the way things are these days in the State Department, anyone over forty who is not married is likely to be accused by McCarthy of being either a lecher or a pervert."

If Secretary Dulles tried to contain McCarthy, or to support officers falsely accused, his efforts escaped the notice of most of the Service. The damage done in the McCarthy "era of book-burning," both to individuals and to the good name of the United States abroad, was tragic.

after country to be nonsense—as the practitioners of diplomacy (in contrast to the planners and administrators) have repeatedly testified. Nor is this view of the efficacy of small staffs an American heresy. A British diplomatist recently declared that "forty years' foreign service has taught me that in diplomacy there is an inverse relationship between numbers and performance. . . . The envoy's is a one-man task; double the team and the results are halved." [11]

What the optimum number of Foreign Service Officers would be, given United States responsibilities in a fast-changing world, is, of course, not easy to say with precision. At the moment, the figure probably falls around twenty-five hundred, as against three thousand seven hundred officers now on the roster.

Certainly with one thousand fewer officers there still should be plenty of administrative elbowroom to take care

---

[11] From Sir John Lomax, as appearing in *The Times* (London) on November 8, 1966. He also observed that "Palmerston, who stayed at home and was served by half a dozen clerks, swayed world events: his present successors have thousands of staff, they rush around the world and nobody heeds," and that "the objection to showy diplomatic establishments is not so much that they are a foreign exchange drain, but that they are ineffective."

In the author's experience, when the Communists of Czechoslovakia forcibly reduced the staff of the American Embassy in Prague by five-sixths—from seventy-eight to thirteen—the efficiency of the mission was multiplied. (See *Farewell to Foggy Bottom*, 1964, chapters IV and X.) See also *The Craft of Diplomacy*, by Sir Douglas Busk (a former British Ambassador). (New York: Praeger, 1967.)

As this book goes to press, word arrives of a campaign initiated by the American Ambassador to Brazil, Mr. John W. Tuthill, to reduce his American staff (now numbering nearly one thousand, the majority from agencies other than the Department of State) by approximately three hundred people. The author, having served as Ambassador to Brazil, wishes his valiant colleague Jack Tuthill all success in his effort to mow down surplus dandelions along Avenida Presidente Wilson, in Rio de Janeiro.

of vacations and home leave, and to assign occasional officers with special aptitudes or interests to the study of esoteric languages, or to a university for an advanced degree in a science relevant to "emerging nations." The State Department should still be able to fill its quota at the postgraduate Government institutions, which are more numerous than the public is aware.[12]

With one thousand fewer officers, the requirements for substantive work could still be met (two or three officers each, in the political and economic sections will usually suffice), and there would be ample talent remaining for

---

[12] The best known are the four so-called War Colleges—the National in Washington, the Army at Carlisle, Pennsylvania, the Naval at Newport, Rhode Island, and the Air War College at Montgomery, Alabama. The author has appeared as lecturer at each of them. All four admit State Department and Foreign Service Officers as students, and each has a State Department Deputy on its faculty.

Conceding that the military will continue to play an important role in foreign affairs, diplomatic graduates of the service schools believe that one of the most valuable dividends of a postgraduate year at a War College is the personal association it brings with colleagues in the armed services. Many of the general and flag officers of today are War College alumni, while their Foreign Service fellow-classmen are Ambassadors. The experience in working together and relaxing together has already made a favorable mark on relations between Pentagon and State.

Not satisfied, however, with helping the soldiers play war games, the State Department now wants to enlarge its own postgraduate production. It has plans to transform the Foreign Service Institute (which for years gave indoctrination to entering officers, together with excellent language training) into an eye-filling educational emporium, providing expanded "mid-career training" for officers with the ink of a dozen years on their commissions, and "senior officer training," where managers who have rarely managed anything larger than a corner suite in Foggy Bottom will explain to Counselors of Embassy how to manage a diplomatic mission.

A communication on this subject, addressed by the author in 1965 to the State Department Deputy serving on the faculty of the Air War College, appears in the Appendix.

Deputy Chief of Mission, for assistants to the Ambassador, for juniors being rotated through Embassy sections for experience, and for officers on loan to the propagandists, the intelligence community, the military establishment, the aid operations, and even the Peace Corps.

With one thousand fewer officers there would still be an ample quota of Foreign Service Officers to fill the "opposite number" positions in the State Department (minus those three hundred jobs "de-designated" as *not* suitable for the Foreign Service).

With one thousand fewer officers, a brisker and more alert corps could be maintained, without the sloppiness that inevitably penetrates an organization that has to invent make-work projects—like the Comprehensive Country Programming System of 1964—in order to convince the Congress, or the public, or itself, how quickly the ship of state would founder without extra hands to polish the brasswork.

In a world where international developments seem to multiply themselves at an ever-increasing pace, it is fashionable to declare that the personnel who suffice today may be inadequate for tomorrow. That is debatable, or at the least a matter for continuing study, which should start from the premise that the roster of the Foreign Service should be kept at the lowest possible figure consistent with getting the job done. That should be coupled with a recruitment policy that will provide a more even flow than heretofore of candidates entering the Foreign Service and a tough but humane "selection out" program that will permit the promotion system to operate.

The other main problem afflicting the Foreign Service is administration: over-administration and lack of continuity. For nearly fifty years before World War II, the machinery was handled by two men only. Alva A. Adee and Wilbur J. Carr were permanent officials of competence and integrity; they proved themselves capable not only of superior accomplishment, but of working harmoniously with successive Secretaries of State, regardless of political party. An incoming Secretary would no more have thought of displacing Adee or Carr than of splashing purple and orange paint on the tesselated corridors of the old State War Navy Building which in happier times housed the American foreign office.[13]

But during the last generation, chief administrators in the State Department have changed with the rapidity of the seasons: business men, politicians, educators, soldiers, technicians, diplomats, bureaucrats, and budgeteers—they have all tried their hands at the controls, sometimes with tolerable and sometimes with deplorable results, but rarely with any show of permanence or continuity.[14]

The most debilitating consequence of poor administration is not the time it consumes or the money it wastes—and it does both—but the stultifying and dispiriting effect it has on a professional service. In the State Department itself, if the Secretary is goaded beyond patience by the computerized dreams of his management experts, he can tell those officials to go jump in the Potomac River—polluted though that stream may be.

Not so the Foreign Service, whose Director General (by legislation an influential official) has been progressively miniaturized, until he is now the whittled-down captive of the Deputy Under Secretary of State for Administration.

---

[13] Two of Adee's highly competent assistants, Mrs. Ruth B. Shipley and Mrs. Blanche Rule Halla, served in the State Department until 1955 and 1965 respectively; Ruth Shipley was Chief of the Passport Division for thirty years, and Blanche Halla was Chief of the Office of Coordination and Review.

[14] An exception was Loy Henderson, whose six years in charge of administration ended with his retirement, with the rank of Career Ambassador, in 1961.

Although the title of Director General persists, authority is lacking; the Director General is now merely one of ten caddies on the administrative golf links, along with the security agents, the chief cipher clerk, the principal of the Institute, the troubadour of Special Programs, and the Director of Budget and Compliance.

The Foreign Service has watched since World War II a steady drift toward mediocrity. This has been exemplified by a freshet of uninspired prose from headquarters, in tone and frequently in content more redolent of the sales pitch of the Griptite Zipper Company than of the foreign office of a great and dignified world power. It has been exemplified by the State Department's *News Letter*, a monthly house organ filled with hortatory aphorisms, squibs about Hands in the Dike, and around-the-world photographs of beaming bureaucrats congratulating other beaming bureaucrats upon their durability or good behavior.[15]

It has been exemplified abroad by a series of shabby and cheese-paring regulations, restricting this or impairing that, and in the area of administration by an effort to establish a janitor's conception of management. The latter possibly derives from one of the less profitable aspects of the Wriston program—the integration into the Foreign Service of many officers of the Staff Corps, who were thereby placed in the false position of out-of-their-depth competition.[16]

---

[15] There is also the *Foreign Service Journal*, a monthly publication of the Foreign Service Association, an unofficial organization. The trouble with the *Journal* is that its directors are officers on active duty, serving in the Department of State, the management of which has not recently been hospitable to criticism.

[16] Happily, this experiment seems to have run its course, and the Staff Corps as a separate but parallel entity within the Foreign Service is being rebuilt. There is need for it, as a respectable and self-respecting unit of foreign affairs. There are needs for budget and fiscal officers, for couriers, for communications specialists, for

Above all, it has been exemplified by the absence of any official of authority in the State Department capable of speaking above a whisper on behalf of the operation and administration of the Foreign Service—a circumstance eloquently noted by two members of the Herter Committee, in a report issued in December 1962.[17] They recommended the creation of the post of Permanent Under Secretary of State, to be number three in the State Department hierarchy, and to be filled from the top echelon of the Foreign Service.

This recommendation that a Permanent Under Secretary, directly responsible to the Secretary of State, be appointed from the Foreign Service is of paramount importance. It is

---

Vice Consuls, for security guards, and for a building superintendent in capitals where the United States has substantial real estate holdings.

There is also a need for a manager or administrator to tie all these activities in an Embassy together, and to keep things in smooth working order. Housekeeping, optimistically christened Management, or Executive Direction, is perhaps more important abroad than it is at home. For an Ambassador, there is no more reassuring knowledge than to recognize that the mechanics of his establishment, including the motor pool and the liquor pool and the commissary, are being operated honestly and efficiently, that rent contracts in the foreign capital, entered into in the Ambassador's name, conform to local law and at the same time protect the interests of the United States, and that the Embassy Residence, visited each year by scores of Congressmen, hundreds of private American citizens, and literally thousands of people of the host country, has the necessary cook, house servants, and gardeners, who will not steal the cigarettes, pocket the ashtrays, or make off with the crested crockery.

The Foreign Service needs a staff corps precisely the way an army needs a quartermaster or an adjutant general. Overseas housekeeping, as a function in support of the conduct of foreign relations, is essential, but it is not diplomacy.

[17] George V. Allen, a retired Career Ambassador, later head of the Foreign Service Institute, and James Rowe, a former White House adviser.

important not only because administration of American
diplomacy has suffered from the over-regulation and petty
regulation of transient outsiders and narrow-gauge insiders,
but also to provide greater continuity within the Department of State itself, especially at times of changing administrations. Although the analogy of diplomacy and the military can readily be overdone, few could imagine the armed
services without a staff organization of their own, or without
a Chief of Staff in the Washington headquarters. Yet for
years the American Government has operated its diplomatic
establishment in precisely those makeshift circumstances.
That it continues to do so is as illogical as it is improvident,
with a debilitating effect on the conduct of foreign relations.

No single step would produce greater dividends in terms
of the efficiency of American diplomacy than the establishment of a Permanent Under Secretary of State, the senior
professional of a career Foreign Service.

The basic challenge facing the American diplomatic
service is, however, more fundamental than administration
or regulations. It is more fundamental than personnel pat-
terns or organization, or "comprehensive country programming," or integration of workers from one sector with
those from another. It involves the question whether the
United States is to have the best diplomatic establishment
of which the American people are capable—an *elite* diplomatic service—or whether the United States is to be served
abroad by an invertebrate bureaucracy where the conception of unselfish professional performance is usurped by
speculation about the possibility of a thirty-hour week, or
anxiety over the availability of corn flakes in the Embassy
commissary.

Second-raters in the hierarchy, sometimes abetted by
Congress, have tried to make *elite* an offensive word—the
opposite, so they declare, of democratic. An elite diplomatic

service has nothing to do with social position or circumstances of birth. By elite is meant an American Foreign Service based on an aristocracy of character, of brains, and of understanding—dedicated to the foreign affairs of the United States. That calls for a competitive, nonpartisan diplomatic service, which disdains anything but the best in human material and in performance, and which rewards its servants with a sense of pride in country and of satisfaction at participating in events significant to the welfare of the American people.

That is what is meant by an elite diplomatic service, and that is the kind of Foreign Service the United States ought to have.

CHAPTER 6

Tools of the Presidency: The
Peripheral Performers ⟨⟨⟨⟨⟨

THIS CHAPTER HAS TO DO WITH THE FOUR CIVILIAN AGENCIES, referred to as the Peripheral Performers, which collaborate most closely with the State Department in overseas operations. They are:

The United States Information Agency (USIA), which is responsible for propaganda and culture, including American libraries in foreign countries;

The Agency for International Development (AID), descendant of the Marshall Plan, now responsible for development projects in backward lands;

The Peace Corps (PC), boys and girls lighting candles in dark places; and

The Central Intelligence Agency (CIA), responsible for this and that, including espionage.

All but CIA, which operates under the National Security Council, are under State Department jurisdiction or policy guidance, but not operational control. State also possesses general jurisdiction—the "overall direction, coordination and supervision" of Government activities overseas—under NSAM-341 of March 4, 1966. (See Chapter 2.)[1]

---

[1] These four agencies do not exhaust the roster of American Government offices with operatives abroad; far from it!

The rationale behind the four principal agencies (and of much of the overseas effort of the American Government, as well) is that the United States, with its responsibilities as a leading world power, needs *action programs* in order to influence the institutions of foreign countries in ways favorable to American purposes.

It should be noted that influencing *institutions* (which includes influencing ideology) is a different proposition from influencing *foreign policy*. Influencing policy is an objective of traditional diplomacy, whereas influencing foreign institutions is a postwar extension of governmental activity. It is at this point that the paths of traditional diplomacy and of the so-called New Diplomacy most often diverge.

With this distinction in mind, let us examine the Peripheral Performers. Let us observe what they are up to in those one hundred and twenty countries with which the United States maintains diplomatic relations—the original

---

A tabulation would include the Departments of Treasury, Agriculture, Commerce, Justice, Labor, Interior, and Health and Welfare, plus the Tariff Commission, the Civil Aeronautics Board, the Federal Aviation Agency, the Veterans Bureau, the National Space Administration, the Atomic Energy Commission, the Budget Bureau, the Social Security Administration, the Smithsonian Institution, the Federal Communications Commission, the Library of Congress, the Maritime Commission, and many many others.

Several of the Executive Departments have multiple representation abroad—separate bureaus, each with its own foreign service—e.g., the Treasury Department with Financial Attachés, Customs and Narcotics representatives, and the Coast Guard.

Most of these representatives occupy office space in Embassy Chanceries; Embassy London, for example, is host to over forty different Washington offices, and its telephone book looks like a New York suburban directory.

This chapter is not concerned with these multitudinous bureaucrats, except to note that they exist and that they clutter up the premises. Some perform useful functions, but a fumigation of the list is long overdue.

United Nations subscribers, plus seventy that have since emerged from their colonial cocoons, becoming by their emergence prime targets for the activists of the New Diplomacy.

The United States Information Agency [2] is the stepchild of the Office of War Information of World War II. Under a Presidential reorganization of 1953, USIA was "established as an independent agency outside the Department of State but subject to its foreign policy guidance." [3] This was in accordance with the wishes of Secretary of State Dulles, who wanted to keep "policy guidance" under his thumb, but was reluctant to have USIA become a part of the State Department itself.

On the record, the USIA mission is "to promote better understanding of the United States among the peoples of the world and to *strengthen cooperative international relations.*" (Italics supplied; what that clause means is anybody's guess, but under it USIA could undertake almost anything, from exterminating wildlife to running an international lottery.)

The primary concern of USIA is, of course, propaganda, called "public information" when used in the first person, at which point it becomes synonymous with "creating a favorable image of the United States." The most imposing operation is the Voice of America (VOA), which broadcasts programs all over the world in most of the languages of the world, with a remarkable stable of multilingual script writers and broadcasters inhabiting the VOA headquarters. Outside the United States, VOA

[2] Known outside the United States as U.S. Information Service (USIS).

[3] See the Herter Committee Report of December 1962: "Personnel of the New Diplomacy," published by the Carnegie Endowment for International Peace, Taplinger Printing Company, Inc., 119 West 57th Street, New York, N.Y.

has a network of transmitting and re-broadcasting facilities, built since World War II.[4]

Because the receptivity of audiences differs, country by country and nationality by nationality, the effectiveness of the Voice of America is not easy to gauge. In Czechoslovakia, where the author served from 1949 to 1952, the impact of VOA was great. There were special reasons: a Western-oriented industrial people, with radio receiving sets in practically every home, suffered a Communist coup d'état in 1948, experiencing thereafter a brutal oppression. Czechoslovakia had close ties with the United States, and to the beleaguered people inside the country the Voice of America brought not only word of relatives and friends, but the fresh air of the lost freedom of the country. Nearly everyone listened.

In other areas, the Voice was less compelling.

In much of the New World there is freedom of information, and adequate press services supply it. There the influence of VOA is limited. Because of small radio-owning audiences in other areas (much of the Far East, South Asia, the Near and Middle East, and Africa) foreign broadcasts have little effect. They are unimportant, for different reasons, in the allied countries of Western Europe.

The extent of jamming of VOA broadcasts to Soviet Russia testifies to the importance the Communists place on preventing foreign propaganda from penetrating the

---

[4] For example, in Greece during the 1950s, VOA had under charter an American Coast Guard Cutter, the *Courier*, which was anchored in the harbor of Rhodes, re-broadcasting Arabic programs to the Near East. For the first few years, the expenditures of the ship's crew were an important addition to the economy of Rhodes, and the islanders were delighted; then the tourists discovered Rhodes, and the vessel became *persona non grata*.

During the same period, USIA maintained a land-based Voice of America station, beamed on Russia, near the northern Greek city of Thessaloniki.

Iron Curtain. But jamming also testifies to a much longer-standing Russian suspicion of foreigners generally, regardless of their ideology or message.

Other forms of mass media and audio-visual stimulants, from movies to magazines in the vernacular, have been tried in various countries, with varying outcomes.

In none of the dozen countries on four continents where the author served—with the exception of Czechoslovakia nearly twenty years ago—was an appreciable dent made by official American propaganda on local thinking, much less on local action. Nor, insofar as could be observed, were any of these countries inclined toward the United States by reason of "government information." In fact, the foreign language editions of *Reader's Digest*, which do not cost the American taxpayers a penny, probably pack as much influence as all the Government propaganda taken together.

Another USIA responsibility is to supply personnel for the "Public Affairs Section" of an Embassy. The job of the Public Affairs Officer (often assisted by a Press Officer) is to keep abreast of local opinion and judiciously to supply the local press with reliable material about the United States. In larger capitals, the Press Officer can provide useful liaison with American correspondents, as well as take on local reporters; this requires a stout constitution.

Cultural operations, responsibility for which USIA shares with the State Department, are long-range and unspectacular, and hence not easy to sell to Congress. On net balance they do promote understanding. Student exchange arrangements are most useful on the graduate level. Those who come to the United States too young often want to stay on as veterinarians to American cattle instead of returning to Addis Ababa to do about the Emperor's lions. The Fulbright program is likewise worth continuing.

American libraries constitute one of the most controversial USIA operations. Immediately after World War II, libraries sprouted like mushrooms, but since the McCarthy campaign of the 1950s, they have fallen upon difficult times. The Senator having rocked the State Department for allegedly harboring "un-American books" in United States Government libraries abroad, the attendant publicity called foreign attention to these enclaves of American culture on alien soil. The demon of nationalism awoke, stimulated by the Communist alarm clock. And from there it was only a short step to attacks on the libraries themselves: burning an American library became the project of any rowdy government wanting to thumb its nose at the United States.[5]

Another tool in the cultural kit is the "bi-national center," which is an institution in a foreign city, initially underwritten by the American Government, but with a local board of directors including citizens of the host country. Bi-national centers sponsor American lecturers, artists, concerts, films, et cetera, give advice about library matters, help screen candidates for Government travel grants in the United States, conduct English lessons, and perform a variety of chores in the fields of education and the arts. Their effectiveness varies widely, depending on the state of relations between the host country and the United States, as well as on the competence of the American

---

[5] Libraries in three of the author's posts illustrate these uncertainties. One (Athens) had been bombed, shortly before my arrival, by Greek students in a pique over Cyprus. Another was gratifyingly popular, especially during winter; it was better heated than most classrooms in the capital and hence became a popular rendezvous for teenagers with time on their hands and dates in the offing. The third, with acres of plate glass, and no fence or railing between the windows and the street, exists in circumstances of mounting hazard; any day we may read of a Spontaneous Demonstration, and of shards of glass knee-deep beside torn American literature.

Cultural Attaché, who is often the Executive Director of the bi-national center.[6]

The State Department made an ill-advised effort in 1965 to blanket into the officer corps of the Foreign Service about eight hundred members of USIS. That would have swollen still further the already over-staffed Foreign Service, and would have diluted its competence by adding many officials not capable of passing individual entry requirements. Moreover, legislation already existed for the entry of those possessing adequate qualifications, and they would have been welcomed by the Foreign Service.[7]

The Agency for International Development (AID) goes back to two of the most successful peacetime projects in which any government in modern times has engaged— the Marshall Plan, which repaired war-torn Western Europe, and the Truman Plan, which enabled Greece and Turkey to rescue themselves from Communism. Both projects were undertaken nearly twenty years ago, and by their success they paved the way for the apparently never-ending boondoggle known as Foreign Aid. How did this come about?

It was reasoned—with many assists from the interested bureaucracy, from certain liberal economists and professors, and from the myriad welfare workers in our generous population—that since Government grants-plus-intervention

---

[6] In modern times the title Cultural Attaché came from Nazi Germany in the 1930s. This gave it an unfortunate connotation, happily not borne out by the American holders of that title.

Good Cultural Attachés, also called Cultural Affairs Officers, are difficult to recruit, since they combine talents not generally developed in a bureaucracy. They are drawn from academic life rather than hatched in the hopper of Government service. They serve as Reserve Officers, often returning eventually to their campuses.

[7] The Senate Foreign Relations Committee blocked the proposal by declining to act on the nominations.

had worked well under the Marshall and Truman Plans, comparable efforts would have equal success everywhere that American technical skill and American dollars could be brought together and focused. It was represented that this would occur regardless of the political or economic development of the beneficiary country, the energy or apathy of the people, or the natural resources available. It was likewise argued that aid programs would invariably result in greater productivity, which would in turn result in a higher standard of living, and finally that a country thus benefited would be less susceptible to Communist penetration.

That is the "aid is a hedge against Communism" argument, which had an immediate appeal to activists inside and outside of government. Moreover, it was catnip to the newly installed Republicans, who in 1953 longed to prove that anything the Truman Administration could do, the Eisenhower Administration could do better. The succeeding Democratic Administration experienced an identical urge in 1961; it produced among other phenomena *Alianza para el Progreso*.

Put another way (by the Herter Committee in 1962), American diplomacy became "committed to assisting developing countries to achieve their aspirations for growth." [8]

---

[8] For an objective treatise on foreign aid, readers are referred to *American Foreign Aid Doctrines* by Professor Edward C. Banfield of Harvard University, published by the American Enterprise Institute for Public Policy Research, 1012 14th Street N.W., Washington, D.C., 1963. This penetrating and comprehensive study of the various theories of foreign aid is preceded by several pungent sentences from President Washington and concludes with an ample bibliography.

See also "Nonsense and Foreign Aid" by Norman A. Bailey of Columbia University, printed in the Columbia University Forum and reprinted in *U.S. News & World Report*, January 9, 1961. Bailey concludes that "the underdeveloped countries want the best of both worlds. They want to have high wages and costly programs of social welfare, and at the same time rapid industrial development. It cannot be done."

In certain circumstances an aid program can provide gratifying results. Those circumstances will include the presence within the aided country of superior human raw material, of a driving ambition for progress shared by both people and government, and of either political sophistication or at the least a political machine capable of staying on the track. To the successful programs in Western Europe, plus Greece and Turkey already mentioned, may be added the programs in Israel, Taiwan, and the Republic of Korea. In each, the American investment was immense, but the results were eventually impressive.

It is when the American Government ventures farther afield, as when it attempts to accelerate social change in backward and "emerging" lands, that Uncle Sam begins stubbing his toe, falling on his face, and miring himself in the quicksands.

Not only did a guiding beacon prove unreliable—primitive and backward countries are rarely capable of utilizing foreign aid except with accompanying waste, corruption, and disorder—but the programs themselves, often confected in Washington by Government spenders imperfectly acquainted with beneficiary countries, were too frequently grandiose, defective, or impractical. The billions of dollars poured out to finance such programs could not possibly have been expended efficiently if each and every one of the administrators had been cast in an angelic mold. The administrators included, to be sure, many unselfish and dedicated workers, inspired by the loftiest of motives. But foreign aid likewise attracted more than its quota of bureaucratic empire builders and happy-go-lucky do-gooders, seeking to alter overnight the age-old customs of foreigners already bewildered by what they saw of the American way of life.

Even the best of the aid programs often collided with

unforeseen obstacles, bruising in the process the citizens and officials of the target countries.

Furthermore, the Congress, which considering the paucity of constituents among beneficiary countries has been remarkably tolerant of successive inflated foreign aid budgets,[9] has nevertheless itself contributed to operational problems. By keeping the programs on a year-to-year basis, the Congress has handicapped forward planning. That has blocked the development of an effective "foreign aid civil service," as well as contributed to the rapid turnover of aid agency directors.[10]

On the other hand, Congress has made important contributions to foreign aid. Reducing inflated budgets has often been accompanied by a demand for the termination

---

[9] For example, the five-billion-dollar Kennedy aid budget. Congressional criticism of that gigantic sum led to the appointment of General Lucius Clay to scrutinize the figures, which he presently reduced to the not insignificant amount of 4.4 billions, declaring in effect that this was the minimum compatible with the national interest. Fortunately, the Congress ignored his expostulations.

[10] The Agency for International Development (AID), successor to the International Cooperation Agency (ICA), which was in turn preceded by the Economic Cooperation Agency (ECA), was established on November 3, 1961, ten months after the inauguration of the Kennedy Administration. It is a semi-autonomous agency within the Department of State—a closer relationship than that of the United States Information Agency, which is outside the State Department.

There are about seven thousand American officials and employees of AID, of whom upwards of four thousand are serving abroad and around two thousand five hundred in Washington. Good results have been obtained by assigning Foreign Service Officers to the AID program directors and deputy directors abroad, and also by the amalgamation within a given Embassy of the aid program with the Economic Section of the diplomatic mission.

Flexibility of operations and of personnel administration should not, however, be confused with amalgamation of personnel, which would not be desirable.

of specific programs which, without such insistence, might well have gone on forever. A favorite dodge of the aid bureaucrats is to agree in principle that a certain program should be terminated, but then to argue that the economic "take-off point" has not quite been reached, and that the program should accordingly be continued (for another one, two, or three years) until the level at which the aided nation is surely capable of underwriting its own progress or generating its own economic momentum has been attained.

Another strategy of the bureaucracy is to agree that a program is now ready to be "phased out," but to maintain that there will be so many loose ends that need tying up, that approximately the same personnel will be needed to take care of the mechanics of the phase-out as were employed before the decision to terminate the operation was made.

In such cases, the aid program personnel are not necessarily insincere. A bureaucrat becomes attached to his project; he is often convinced that his program is on the verge of succeeding, and conversely that unless it receives just one more injection of foreign aid funds "all that has been accomplished thus far is in danger of being lost." By the same token, few AID personnel will ever admit that a given program has been a failure.

Again, Congress has been much more insistent than the Executive (or the bureaucracy) that minimal standards of behavior for beneficiaries of foreign aid should be established. As described in Chapter 3, Executives usually resist Congressional attempts to lay down conditions, on the grounds that future developments or unexpected contingencies require the greatest possible freedom of action; Congress, in contrast, believes that it should at least be regarded as bad form for a petitioner for millions of dollars' worth of aid to spit in Uncle Sam's eye, or to burn down his

USIS library, by way of emphasizing his appreciation of the generosity of the American people.[11]

In addition to projects which it undertakes in its own name, AID likewise enters into contracts with private institutions. For instance, one of the most successful projects in Brazil was the founding of a School of Business Administration in the city of São Paulo, financed by AID but carried out by Michigan State University. Again, medical programs often make use of the services of the Pan American Health Organization or the World Health Organization. These arrangements have the advantage of restraining the bureaucracy from invading or dominating the scene, and of putting programs in the hands of professionals, who will not resist going away once a program is finished.

The Agency for International Development maintains close relations with lending agencies such as the Export Import Bank, the Inter-American Development Bank, the World Bank, the International Monetary Fund, the International Development Association, et cetera, which are tapped to underwrite both handouts as well as programs regarding which it is deemed politic to create the illusion that the beneficiary may eventually pay something on account. A special kind of prose, known to semanticists as "Who Is Kidding Whom" has been developed to describe these travel-today-pay-later operations.[12]

---

[11] In the malarial and intransigent Republic of Guinea, the recipients of millions of dollars in various forms of American largesse responded in November 1966 by sacking the American Embassy residence, closing the USIS library, declaring several members of the Embassy staff *persona non grata*, and expelling the Peace Corps.

"United States aid," declared the official Guinean newspaper, "is economic blackmail. Pack your bags, Americans. . . ."

[12] Here is a sample:

AID's loan to *Ultrafertil*, guaranteed by the Blank Government,

The following titles, chosen at random from a recent public relations bulletin of the Agency for International Development, further illustrate the scope of current operations:

"AID approves Food for Peace to help grain-short Ghana."

"AID pact with Bureau of Customs aims to improve port supervision in Vietnam."

"Food for Peace to help settle farmers and nomads in Afghanistan."

"Food for Freedom will help improve water in India."

"17,469 tons of Food for Peace will fight illiteracy in Brazil."

(Note: the difference between Food for *Peace* in Afghanistan and Food for *Freedom* in India remains unexplained.)

The Peace Corps originated early in the Kennedy Administration, amid much popular acclaim but little critical appraisal. The name itself was beguiling: the words "Peace Corps" took the play away from Russia, which for years had tried to identify "peace" with Communist propaganda.

From the outset, missionary zeal was invoked, and the Peace Corps focused on youth. Soon it became a sort of 20th-century Children's Crusade, but with better transportation, medical facilities, and nutrition than Pope Innocent

---

will be repaid in dollars within fifteen years, including a five-year grace period, with annual interest at 5½%. Under an alternate plan, the Blank Government may exercise its option of repaying the AID loan in dollars within forty years, including a ten-year grace period. Interest during the grace period would be at the annual rate of one percent; thereafter it would be 2½%.

(As between fifteen years at 5½%, or ten years at one percent plus thirty years at 2½%, the borrowing government is obviously facing a manageable quandary.)

III was able to furnish. The Peace Corps likewise soon boasted a far more effective public relations apparatus.

Many candidates were undoubtedly fired with a desire to improve the condition of people less fortunately fixed than most of the citizens of the United States. Others aspired to visit places romantically remote. Still others were probably bored with the idea of selling insurance, or apathetic about entering the armed service. But missionary zeal was the dominant feature of the public image. Moreover, the Peace Corps fitted comfortably into the concept of a junior-league foreign aid program, even though the notion of the "white man's burden," which is inescapably inherent in that concept, had been deleted from the Potomac book of maxims as redolent of colonialism.

Foreign demand for Peace Corps Volunteers did not generate spontaneously. Demand was stimulated by a campaign employing the techniques of Madison Avenue. These portrayed the inhabitants of undeveloped lands waving welcome mats, woven from pandanus leaves, and cheering.[13]

Today there are no less than fifteen thousand Peace Corps Volunteers, serving in fifty backward or "emerging" nations. Their cost in 1967 was one hundred and ten million dollars, or approximately one-half of the cost of operating the entire State Department and Foreign Service.[14] The

---

[13] Even the distant Mediterranean was propositioned. Embassy Athens was directed to sound out the Greek Government, to the tenor of "How would you like a batch of Peace Corps Volunteers? They are free, you know." Few Hellenes since Homer having answered such a query except in the affirmative, Greece was duly represented in Washington as panting to have the Acropolis face-lifted by Volunteers. (An unregenerate bureaucrat later scratched the project. The irony of having the Cradle of Civilization rocked by teenagers finally daunted even Foggy Bottom.)

[14] The 1967 State Department budget was $387 million, but forty percent of that was earmarked for such things as United Nations, contributions to U.S.-Mexico water control, cultural ex-

Peace Corps comprises yet another bureaucracy in Washington, plus a growing Peace Corps managerial staff abroad. The latter officials, ensconced in embassies and eager for diplomatic privileges and immunities, are there to administer the Volunteers, who themselves are scattered about in successive hinterlands, from the Congo Basin to the windswept uplands of the Andean sierra. The Volunteers live austerely; the managers receive up to $25,000 a year for administering them.

The Peace Corps raises the basic question of the propriety of having the American Government undertake missionary activities abroad. Until 1961 it was the consensus that missionary work is a matter of private conscience and individual effort, conducted mainly through churches. Although the operations of the Peace Corps have been reasonably free from criticism, this fundamental question remains. With it is the question whether this abundant crusading zeal, now primarily employed toward influencing primitive foreign cultures, might not more appropriately and more profitably be applied to depressed areas within the United States itself.

It may be more colorful and exciting to work with the Ibos of Nigeria than with their grandchildren in the ghettos of Los Angeles and Harlem, but which activity would be better for the United States remains a pertinent query.

Granted that a majority of the Peace Corps Volunteers are sincere in their efforts, and that they themselves, having found an outlet for American idealism, may be benefited by the experience of trying to solve difficult or insoluble alien problems, the extent of the Peace Corps impact on the target countries is less than overwhelming. Foreign

---

changes, et cetera. The regular program of the State Department and the Foreign Service comes to about $225 million, as against $110 million for the Peace Corps.

customs and cultures, including those that militate against what Americans call progress, are too firmly embedded to be shaken loose by enthusiastic youngsters, no matter how enterprising or well-intentioned. Even if the Peace Corps were expanded to one hundred thousand Volunteers and set to doing everything from melting the ice of Antarctica to freezing it again in Greenland, the penguins and the sea lions would probably revert the next week to their immemorial customs, unhygienic though those habits might be.

And even in the most productive of Peace Corps circumstances, the effect of their activities abroad is unquestionably less than it would be if the same young people concentrated the same dedication and zeal—not to forget those same millions of dollars—on issues that confront the citizens living in underdeveloped or "emerging" areas of the United States.

From the Trojan Horse to the Bay of Pigs is a long span, but the business of espionage—or, as former CIA Director Allen Dulles puts it, "the craft of intelligence"—is as old as recorded history. Such activities in the United States have had their ups and downs.[15]

In this century, the low point for American intelligence activities was probably reached in 1929, when Secretary of State Stimson, with the high-minded but impractical observation that "gentlemen do not read each other's mail," suppressed the code-breaking operations which since World War I had been lodged in the State Department. Stimson's

---

[15] For a survey of the Central Intelligence Agency, see *The Craft of Intelligence*, by Allen Dulles. (New York: Harper & Row, 1963.)

Those interested in the beginnings of espionage in the United States and in the important part played by it during the American Revolution are referred to *A Peculiar Service*, by Corey Ford. (Boston: Little, Brown, 1965.)

action handicapped American intelligence during the crucial decade of the 1930s.[16]

Since 1947, with the creation of the Central Intelligence Agency, American espionage has definitely been up, notwithstanding the doubts that arose after the unsuccessful effort to topple the Castro regime in 1961. And it is likely to remain up, for at least as long as the Cold War, which after over twenty years shows few signs of thawing.[17]

In broad terms, intelligence activity covers two adjacent areas: overt operations having to do with the collection and interpretation of information, and clandestine operations, which by different means pursue the same end, that is, foreknowledge of the intentions and capabilities of an enemy. To the extent that CIA engages in the first activity—overt collection of information abroad—it obviously duplicates, or at any rate supplements, a basic diplomatic function. Gathering information abroad, and interpreting that information for the purpose of assisting the formulation of foreign policy, remains a fundamental attribute of the State Department and the Foreign Service.

Clandestine operations are important both positively, as

----

[16] An account of American cryptanalytic activities is found in *The American Black Chamber* by Herbert O. Yardley. (Indianapolis: Bobbs-Merrill, 1931.) Yardley, a code clerk in the State Department when World War I broke out, later headed the secret unit which Secretary Stimson suppressed. Being out of a job, Yardley wrote a book about his work and experiences, publication of which today would be an illegal disclosure of sensitive and highly classified material.

[17] It would be difficult to improve on the following statement of the problem, from Dulles's *Craft of Intelligence*, already cited:

"In the Soviet Union we are faced with an antagonist who has raised the art of espionage to unprecedented height, while developing the collateral techniques of subversion and deception into a formidable political instrument of attack. No other country has ever attempted this on such a scale. These operations . . . go on in times of so-called thaw and under the guise of coexistence with the same vigor as in times of acute crisis. . . ."

contributing to the same foreknowledge ("one peek is as good as two finesses"), and negatively, in the sense that the failure of a covert project may have embarrassing repercussions—viz., the shooting down of the American U-2 spy plane over Russia in 1959, and the ill-fated Bay of Pigs operation in Cuba two years later.

The question is not, then, whether espionage is moral, or proper, or the right thing to do, but how the intelligence apparatus shall be operated, to whom and to what extent it shall be responsible, and how it shall be controlled. And control entails decisions about the value of the assets to be risked to achieve a given objective, the establishment of priorities, and above all the relationship between the junior partner, intelligence activity, and the senior partner, diplomacy.

It is here that much of the argument has arisen and the criticism has been aimed. It has been charged that CIA has become a law unto itself, a vast invisible government within the Government, and that far from acting in junior partnership with diplomacy, CIA has usurped the functions of a pusillanimous State Department and a fumbling Foreign Service. That is an extreme view. Although examples are cited,[18] about the only things they prove are that the Central Intelligence Agency is probably over-staffed (like most of the rest of the Washington bureaucracy), that it has produced an occasional free-wheeling eager beaver, and that both the State Department itself and certain Ambassadors in foreign countries have failed to show adequate leadership or to exert sufficient authority.

Certainly there is no question at the present time where

---

[18] For example, the suppression for more than a year of the State Department's *Foreign Service List*, in deference to a CIA complaint that publication of the List (which has been appearing for half a century) jeopardized the cover of CIA personnel serving in diplomatic missions.

the authority lies, if the State Department has the strength and character to use it.

Liaison between State and CIA is now reasonably good. Few problems exist regarding overt operations in foreign countries. Clandestine projects are not supposed to be undertaken without the knowledge of the Ambassador concerned. That does not mean that a Chief of Mission should expect to be supplied with the details of a specific undertaking. But an Ambassador should be aware of what it is sought to achieve, and he should agree that the objective is worth what is being hazarded, including possible deterioration of bilateral relations if the undertaking fails.[19]

To conclude with a personal observation, the author had fifteen years in close association with CIA personnel abroad. He was served by mature, sophisticated, and competent officials, whose contribution to the achievements of the missions concerned was substantial.

In dedicating the new CIA headquarters in Virginia in November 1961, a scant seven months after the Bay of Pigs embarrassment, President Kennedy remarked to Allen Dulles, "Your successes are unheralded, your failures are trumpeted . . . [but] I am confident that in the future you will continue to merit the appreciation of our country, as you have in the past."

---

[19] The U-2 flights represent a case in point. They produced highly significant information, over a considerable period of time (during which the operation was, of course, known to the Soviet Government), but when the U-2 was shot down, the project did adversely affect Soviet-United States relations. It was seized upon by Khrushchev as an instrument wherewith to wreck the summit conference.

As perspective lengthens, it is not the recklessness of the U-2 operation in terms of bilateral relations that is vulnerable to criticism, but the *timing* of that particular flight, so close to the scheduled summit meeting, which presented the Russians with their opportunity.

Conclusions about the Peripheral Performers:

A belief that it is possible for one country to modify the institutions of another country has some validity—at least, up to a point, and depending on the country—but the extent to which it is desirable for the United States to engage in that sort of warfare is open to question. "Up to a point" and "depending on the country" are illustrative of the gremlins lurking in the shadows, ready to pounce on an unwary premise. Furthermore, generalizations about political behavior that are vulnerable to variants provide dangerous political footing. Related assumptions soon become fuzzy with unanswered queries and wishful thinking.

For instance, how long is a target country, having been wooed by pretty phrases or coaxed by rising expectations, going to stay influenced, once the phrases have ceased to echo and the expectations have subsided? Again, who can compute the rebellion rate of pensioners and pawns, once the subsidy has been withdrawn or the pawn ticket presented for redemption? Then, too, if the American Government refrains from influencing another country, is a power hostile to the United States likely to succeed in doing so, to the detriment of American interests?

True, Castro in Cuba mortgaged himself to Russia, but where are the statistics showing how much it has cost the Kremlin to keep that vindictive and interminable orator in voice, month after month and year after year? And how do we know whether the Moscow comrades still think that Castro is worth it?

The tenor of these questions indicates that the "action programs" so cherished by the planners are skirmishes or campaigns in the Cold War. They constitute an American response to a Communist threat, real or imagined. (Real, to be sure, in Santo Domingo in 1965.) These responses are frequently buttressed by the conviction that in the absence of a United Nations game warden, the institutions of a neighbor are fair game for the Potomac poacher. They are strengthened by the innate evangelism of the American people, who are rarely more bubbly and enthusiastic than when they are out playing Daniel Boone or Davy Crockett in someone else's zoological garden.[20]

The existence of a foreign aid program, no matter how carefully conceived or lavishly subsidized, cannot guarantee that the beneficiary country will become more productive, less vulnerable to Communist penetration, more dedicated to the purposes of the free world, or less hungry than it was before. Least of all does the existence of an aid program guarantee that the assistance will be used wisely, or that the recipient country will be grateful to the United States.

The foreign aid program should therefore be trimmed. Not abandoned, for that would be to jettison a tool which "up to a point, and depending on the country" can sometimes be helpful. It can be helpful as an *adjunct* to traditional diplomacy, but not as a substitute for it.

If the American people are disposed to hazard two or three billion dollars a year, against odds of, say, five to one that a substantial proportion of each appropriation will either go up in smoke or down the drain, then perhaps in terms of the gross national product of the United States that is not too great an annual extravagance. Provided, of course, that the American people do not kid themselves about the odds, or expect to hit a jackpot more often than once in a good many tugs at the sleeve of the one-armed bandit of international relations.

---

[20] Witness the popularity of that mother-and-brat cartoon over the caption: "Eat it, dear; it's broccoli." Even though we conveniently forget that Mother's Scowling Treasure—prototype of an emerging nation receiving foreign aid—rudely retorts, "I say it's spinach, and I say the hell with it."

So much for influencing our neighbors' institutions.

For over one hundred and fifty years after independence, the United States managed to get along without Government propaganda. That activity started about thirty years ago, as a reply to Communist Russia and Nazi Germany. Propaganda became a weapon of subversion in World War II, and propaganda disguised as information was continued by the United States thereafter, but without referendum or popular debate. To this day, no real investigation has been made—except by bureaucrats who are interested parties—of the proposition: American Government propaganda is (or is not) a waste of money and effort.

Such an investigation should start from the premise that although it may be possible to gild the lily, the result invariably looks like a flower with gold paint on it, and that the most convincing national image is projected by the way in which a country handles its own affairs. Nothing—literally nothing—takes the place of the picture of a country coping with its destiny by governing itself efficiently. It is furthermore remarkable how quickly that picture registers on the consciousness of the rest of the world, without drum-beating, hocus-pocus with mirrors, or official propaganda.

Conversely, when troubles fill the air, and one race snarls at another race, and unbalanced budgets follow one another, it is naive indeed to think that Government propaganda is the answer to the problem of impressing the friends of the United States. Far less will propaganda fetch to our side the neutrals and the uncommitted nations. And since the neutrals and the uncommitted are among the principal targets —even though the value of their good opinion is often over-rated—that is a very considerable limitation on the usefulness of propaganda.

A substantial part of the American propaganda apparatus

will therefore appear to represent costly futility, and the elaborate edifice of the United States Information Agency ought to be taken apart, with only such pieces salvaged and reassembled as experience has shown to be useful. Those should include more of the cultural and exchange programs than those of the lily-gilders and magaphone wielders.

As for the Central Intelligence Agency, the artisans of the craft of intelligence will be with us for a long time. It is the responsibility of diplomacy to take advantage of their activities, but not to be dominated by them.

The personnel roster of CIA is probably thirty or forty percent too large, including personnel attached to American Embassies abroad. Reductions, pursuant to recommendations elicited from each Ambassador concerned, should be made.

And with respect to the accountability of CIA to Congress, the Committee on Foreign Relations should have an important voice about what goes on in that impressive headquarters on the south bank of the Potomac.

Lastly, the Peace Corps. The Children's Crusade should quietly go out of business.

CHAPTER 7

Diplomats and Warriors

OUTSIDE THE DEPARTMENT OF STATE, NO AGENCY OF GOV-
ernment has a greater stake in foreign affairs than the military, who, when diplomacy is unable to contain the flames of
international controversy, have to cope with the conflagration. Only since World War II, however, has American
military participation in the conduct of foreign affairs sur-
vived the termination of hostilities. After previous wars the
soldiers went home, and the diplomats went back to work.
But so widespread was the conflict a quarter of a century
ago that diplomatic activity became almost everywhere an
accessory to military operations, and that generated a momentum on the part of the military which persisted long
after the guns became silent.

Disregarded and denigrated by President Roosevelt, and
often pushed around by generals with more gift for noise
than for negotiation, the Foreign Service was on short rations during World War II. Furthermore, the military not
only engaged in diplomacy, they developed a voracious ap-
petite for it, even though their aptitude for diplomatic
activity was often on a par with the talent of a diplomat
for piloting a bomber or navigating a destroyer. It was not,

indeed, until 1956, eleven years after Germany and Japan surrendered, that the American Ambassador was again recognized as the ranking representative of his Government abroad.[1]

More important in the sweep of history than the soldier aspiring to be a diplomat is the fact that victory in 1945 was not followed by peace. Today, in the third decade after Pearl Harbor, the Cold War continues, although the occupation of former enemy territory has long since ended. The containment of Communism remains the cornerstone of American foreign policy, and to implement that policy requires continuing military strength as well as commitments to use it. For the United States this uneasy period has involved two shooting wars—Korea and Vietnam—plus crises uncounted; above all, it has meant the maintenance of a resolute military presence, at home and in many foreign countries.

American missions and bases abroad are parts of the worldwide operation called military aid, whereby the United States seeks to strengthen its friends by furnishing them with the sinews of defense: hardware of all categories and descriptions, from warships to tanks, guns, and airplanes, plus technical assistance and training in their use, and collaboration in military planning. Military aid deals with tangibles, which are subject to more effective control than welfare projects and give-away programs that presuppose a higher degree of managerial sophistication than sometimes exists in recipient countries. In "developing countries" the military caste often dominates the scene, containing at times the only element capable of "making a government work." Thus the establishment of cordial relations with the military may be important politically, in addition to pro-

---

[1] By Executive Order of President Eisenhower. See Chapter 2.

viding arms with which to combat subversion or aggression.[2]

With over half the American budget today devoted to defense, the influence of the military must inevitably be pervasive. At the top, that influence is exerted in the relationship among the President and the Secretaries of Defense and State, plus the National Security Council and the Joint Chiefs of Staff. In the hierarchy of the Department of State, liaison with the Pentagon is maintained primarily by the Under Secretary of State and by the Deputy Under Secretary for Political Affairs, and on lower levels by Assistant Secretaries and through committees and officers assigned by Pentagon to State, and vice versa.

Leaving aside the formulation of high policy, and also the daily and hour-by-hour association between Foggy Bottom and the military establishment in Washington, there are four general areas of activity where diplomats and warriors work most closely together.

The first is the area of the graduate-level service schools, headed by the National War College. These institutions were discussed in Chapter 5. In them, military-diplomatic liaison is fruitful and continuing.

Second, there is the presence of Armed Service Attachés in American Embassies abroad. That is the traditional State-and-military relationship where each Ambassador has on his staff Army, Navy, and Air Force Attachés, who act as aides to the Chief of Mission in ceremonial capacity and as

---

[2] Critics of military aid complain that it fosters militarism at the expense of democracy, that it perpetuates domination by the military caste, and that it paves the way for a dictator under whom the inhabitants of a country may fare little better than they would under Communist oppression. (Trujillo, late dictator of the Dominican Republic, is often cited.) They point out further that dictators are forever trying to play off one side against the other, seeking arms from each, or using their weapons to keep fellow-citizens in bondage.

advisers to the Embassy in its day-by-day operations.[3] Additionally, each Attaché is accredited by his Chief of Staff in Washington to the foreign Chief of Staff in the host country; the Attaché is expected to establish cordial relations with his opposite numbers in the foreign military establishment, precisely as the civilian officers of the Embassy do with their colleagues in the host government.

Attachés reach their foreign posts better equipped than they used to. Having plenty of manpower, the armed services choose Attachés well in advance, and assign them for one year of language and other special training in the United States before sending them overseas. Moreover, since the war, an effort has been made to attract higher-caliber candidates—officers who are not terminating their careers with attaché gold braid on their shoulders, but enriching their future usefulness by the experience of an Embassy tour of duty.

Various problems remain. Notwithstanding stimulating aspects of Attaché service, an aroma of the "society colonel" still clings to the job, discouraging candidates. The pace of technological change in weaponry is so rapid that others are reluctant to spend two or three years in a remote capital or a militarily backward country for fear of falling behind on the promotion list. (It is a fact that comparatively few former Attachés reach general or flag rank.)

Many Attaché offices are too large, with all three armed services represented in a single Embassy, where one "Armed Forces Attaché" (or "Defense Attaché"), possibly sup-

---

[3] An Attaché airplane is likewise a valuable adjunct to a diplomatic mission, especially in countries where distances are great or travel facilities deficient. (Regulations regarding use of the plane have frequently been unduly restrictive. It is hoped the Air Force has new equipment in mind, once the dwindling supply of obsolete C-47s is cannibalized.)

ported by one junior Assistant from each of the other two services, would be more economical and efficient.[4]

The intelligence aspect of Attaché duty both attracts and complicates, especially since the creation in Washington in 1961 of the Defense Intelligence Agency—yet another tentacle of the growing bureaucracy, which notwithstanding the guarded optimism of former CIA Director Allen Dulles [5] seems more likely to wrap itself around future Attaché operations than to content itself with the passive role of preparing estimates and evaluations. Since Attachés pursue "military intelligence," and CIA seeks "political intelligence," there is theoretically no conflict between them; but like many copybook distinctions, they often collapse in practice. Since a flair for intelligence work is not always a component of the military mind, collisions between Attaché and CIA personnel abroad are not infrequent, with the Ambassador called upon to separate patriotic but frustrated contestants.

On balance, however, and barring the overstaffing aforesaid, Attaché service has improved since World War II, keeping pace with improved liaison between State and Defense in other areas.[6]

---

[4] Service rivalry plays its part in this. One service dislikes to concede that in a given foreign country another service is more important than it is; each service accordingly demands its own Attaché.

In Czechoslovakia, Attaché personnel on the author's arrival totaled thirty-three in a staff of eighty Americans. In Greece a decade later, the Attaché roster numbered no less than seventy-seven officers and men. Two or three would have sufficed in Prague, and half a dozen in Athens.

[5] See Dulles's *The Craft of Intelligence*, p. 47.

[6] Not a part of Attaché service, but deserving of mention before leaving the subject, is the important contribution of the Marine Corps in providing a guard detachment for each of over one hundred and twenty American Embassies. These detachments of se-

MAAGs, Missions, and military bases. In Latin America, after World War I, there was a scramble to replace German and other European military missions with personnel from the United States. These missions set a pattern for the "Military Assistance Advisory Groups" known as MAAGs, which proliferated in other parts of the world soon after the second world war on a greatly expanded scale. The MAAGs perform twin assignments: instructing the host government in the use of American military hardware and equipment, and aiding in staff planning against contingencies.[7]

The MAAG commanding officer is usually a two-star general, assisted by naval and air components. Unlike the Attachés, who are part of the Ambassador's diplomatic staff and members of his official family, the relationship of the MAAG to an Embassy has a built-in ambiguity capable of producing friction. The MAAG commandant belongs to the Pentagon, communicating with and responsible to Washington through the military chain of command. But at the same time he is subject to the jurisdiction of the Ambassador as the representative of the President in the foreign country concerned. The MAAG chief meets with Embassy personnel as a member of the Ambassador's

---

lected enlisted men, each in charge of a veteran Sergeant, are responsible for the physical security of Chancery premises, an exacting undertaking. In the case of large diplomatic missions, as many as thirty Marines may be involved, whereas half a dozen suffice at smaller posts.

Although a cordial State-Marine Corps relationship goes back many decades—witness the famous Legation Guard in Peking, as well as the frequent services of Marines in the Caribbean—the present responsibility has been exercised only since World War II.

[7] And incidentally keeping an eye on the uses to which American weapons are put. For instance, when Portugal, a NATO ally, used American airplanes against disaffected tribesmen in Portuguese Guinea, the United States Government remonstrated.

"country team," and his annual plans are submitted to the Embassy for endorsement. Beyond that, a MAAG chief is largely on his own, and his operations can exert a considerable effect on bilateral relations.

Military Assistance Advisory Groups are functioning in countries allied with the United States all the way from NATO to Thailand, Taiwan, and Korea.

In Latin America, military training operations are still conducted by Missions. The principal difference between a Mission and a MAAG is that in the former the American personnel are present by contract with the host government, which often pays not only expenses but also extra compensation for the officers concerned, as well as granting them diplomatic privileges and exemptions. Some Missions have been operating for many years—the Naval Missions to Peru and Brazil, for example, were established during the 1920s—and a substantial backlog of shared experience and goodwill has resulted. (See also Chapter 12 on Latin America.)

Unlike MAAGs and Missions, American *bases* on foreign soil have no official status in the host country, except that they were established in accordance with a prior permission or agreement, usually negotiated on the diplomatic level. Bases exist to perform some specific military function, sometimes as a part of a multilateral arrangement of alliance, but more frequently as a cog in the United States military machine overseas. Base personnel may be limited to a handful of officers and a score of enlisted men, or the complement may total thousands, plus dependents, post exchanges, schools and recreational facilities, hospitals, chapels, and all the paraphernalia of Little America abroad.[8]

---

[8] There are literally scores of American bases scattered about the world, some dating from World War II.

In Panama, immediately after that war, the United States sought

Military bases create diplomatic problems—problems that
are inherent in the presence on alien soil of lusty young
Americans who are only casually acquainted with the language, culture, and customs of the host country, but highly
solvent in terms of local purchasing power. Jurisdiction over
base personnel is governed by "status of forces agreements"
(SOFA in military parlance), and the interpretation and
application of those agreements provide headaches galore
for the American Embassies situated in host countries.[9]

Many incidents that occur involve the automobiles of
service personnel—a problem that is exacerbated by the
liberal automobile policy of the American military. Bases
are always swarming with American cars, many in decrepit
condition, and off-duty young men depart in them for the
center of things, precisely as they do in the United States.
The difficulty is that they are not in the United States;
abroad, every automobile incident is a public relations time
bomb, ticking away beneath the edifice of goodwill between
the United States and an ally. Every such case is susceptible

unsuccessfully to acquire over one hundred base sites in that republic alone. In France, twenty years later, when de Gaulle served
his eviction notice on the United States in 1966, there were more
than forty American bases operating. They included supply depots,
airstrips, port facilities, and communications centers—a vast investment in plant and installations, part of which has been transferred,
part sold, and part abandoned.

[9] SOFA agreements are individually negotiated, country by country, and hence differ in details. They generally distinguish between
offenses against the laws of the host country occurring while on
duty (or in the performance of duty), and those that take place
while off duty. In the first case, the American military retains jurisdiction; in the second, the host country tries the alleged offender
in accordance with local law and, if a conviction results, can sentence him to a local jail. Thus a military courier, proceeding with
dispatches from an American base to the American Embassy in the
capital, is immune from local jurisdiction if he has an accident,
whereas the same enlisted man, driving the same route off duty one
hour later, may be subject to the jurisdiction of the country.

of misrepresentation or exploitation by the Communist press, or by the political opposition to the Government in power, seeking to embarrass the administration.[10]

Another source of friction is the Post Exchange—no way having yet been devised to keep cigarettes and nylon stockings, not to forget cosmetics and nightgowns, from being presented by soldiers to what the military describe as "indigenous female personnel." Post exchanges were initially established in places where retail goods were either scarce or nonexistent—devastated Europe in 1945, for example. Over twenty years later, there is scant excuse for post exchanges in Europe, although possibly more in primitive areas, or in countries where the domestic toothpaste removes enamel, or the talcum powder smells of patchouli, or razor blades and chewing gum are hard to come by.[11]

---

[10] In countries where there are large numbers of American military personnel, the Embassy maintains fulltime liaison officers to handle cases arising under SOFA agreements. They seek to settle cases out of court, to dampen adverse publicity, and through the Foreign Office to persuade the host Government to waive jurisdiction in cases of minor misdemeanors and infractions.

(The principal accomplice in "Americans, Go Home" campaigns is the serviceman's jalopy.)

[11] The author's campaign against post exchanges was not notably successful. Complaint to Washington having been registered by the Embassy on behalf of the host Government against the sale by the PX of French perfume, German cameras, Japanese toys, Belgian shotguns, Italian embroidery, and British textiles, as well as the failure of the PX to stock local commodities—all that to the detriment of national commerce and the inflammation of national pride —a team from PX headquarters hundreds of miles away was flown to the capital, where they remained several weeks.

Their report was illuminating. As to cameras and shotguns, they predicted that the "dollar gap" would soon cure that (to the disappointment of traveling Congressmen, seeking bargains). But as for stocking local commodities—very difficult. "Local shoes," they declared, "are sturdy, but squeak. And local brassieres do not fit American women. . . ."

These harassments are the pinpricks present in a relationship that is inherently awkward—the presence of soldiers of one nation quartered in peacetime on the territory of another. When it is the agreed policy of two governments to endorse that alien presence, then forbearance must be the word, and it is the duty of diplomacy to contribute what it can toward tolerance and understanding.

Across the lengthening years since World War II, the interests of the United States have probably been better served by military aid, including even such difficult military arrangements as bases, than they have by nonmilitary aid, with all its waste, inefficiency, false premises, and false promises. There have undoubtedly been exceptions, but at least military aid has an intelligible objective. The trick of statesmanship is to find the prescription that fits the country, be it a blend of civil and military aid, or one or the other, or neither—depending on circumstances that shift from year to year and sometimes almost from day to day.

Continuing debate of these issues indicates not only their importance, but also the desirability of a selective approach to the problems of collaboration and assistance, where "policy guidance" must be flexible to avoid becoming a strait-jacket.

The fourth and last phase of State-Pentagon association occurs in a war area—Korea yesterday and Vietnam today—where diplomacy is subordinate to fighting. Here the diplomatic effort supplements and supports the military effort, and the Ambassador plays a role secondary to that of the military commander.[12]

---

[12] This situation prevailed in extreme form during World War II, where the diplomatic contribution was at times almost obliterated. That war saw, however, the development of a useful official called the "Political Adviser"—POLAD in the command hierarchy. POLADs were Foreign Service Officers, usually of senior rank, who

Within the concept of diplomacy in support of a war effort, there are interesting contrasts between the State-Pentagon relationship in Korea fifteen years ago, and in Vietnam today.

Embassy Seoul between 1950 and 1953 was a comparatively compact operation. Its primary task was the relationship with the venerable President Rhee, who was convinced that the proposed armistice with the Communists was iniquitous, and who repeatedly threatened to upset the negotiations. Those negotiations in turn were conducted on a military, not diplomatic, plane. Moreover, the Korean war was theoretically and technically a United Nations undertaking. The United States supplied, it is true, over ninety-five percent of the effort, but there were sixteen United Nations allies, and the blue-and-white United Nations flag flew over headquarters.

Toward the American campaign in Vietnam, in contrast, the majority of the now far more numerous United Nations members are either lukewarm or openly hostile. Moreover in Vietnam the United States operates in its own name, with a handful of individual allies.

In Korea, an immense nonmilitary aid program was inaugurated a year before the 1953 armistice. Until after the armistice, however, that program operated as a de-

---

were attached to military commands, both ashore and afloat. Their function was to provide diplomatic and political counsel to the commanding general or admiral with respect to a wide range of nonmilitary problems affecting both the inter-Allied relationship and, later, relations with the enemy.

Probably the best known POLAD was Robert Murphy, Political Adviser to General Eisenhower during the war and to General Lucius Clay in Berlin shortly thereafter. Murphy's distinguished career is described in *Diplomat Among Warriors* (Garden City, N.Y.: Doubleday, 1964).

Political Advisers are still being assigned.

pendency of the military command, and not as an Embassy or State Department responsibility. In Vietnam a comparable program, on an even larger scale and with even broader social implications, functions under Embassy Saigon jurisdiction, exercised by a politically potent Ambassador, assisted by Deputy Ambassadors and a huge civilian staff.[13]

---

[13] To some extent, these contrasting operations reflect differences in the peoples involved. In Korea the United States was dealing with a tough, hard, self-reliant people, with a history of independence, and with a determined President who was a genuine leader. Korea was and remains a valued ally of the United States. In Vietnam the United States is dealing with a limp, politically quarrelsome people, with little demonstrated capacity for self-government, at times apparently almost indifferent to efforts to rescue them from Communist domination.

CHAPTER 8

A Day with the American Ambassador, or What Makes an Embassy Tick 🪶

THERE IS NO SUCH THING AS A TYPICAL EMBASSY. THEREIN lies some of the charm of diplomacy for professional diplomats, as well as some of its frustration. An Ambassador's life can be one of infinite variety, but what is effective procedure at Post A may have little relevance to operations at Post B, in a different continent. Or even at Post C on the same continent. The successful ambassadorial approach in one country may have to be abandoned in the next, where a whole new set of ground rules may be in operation.[1]

Moreover, an Ambassador, to a degree not approached by an executive of comparable responsibility in any other profession, can be at the mercy of forces over which he exercises little control—his own government, and the government of the country to which the Ambassador is accredited.

---

[1] An effort was recently made by the State Department to divide diplomatic missions into those established in sophisticated countries, where traditional diplomacy is not yet in disrepute, and those functioning in countries dedicated to "internal development," where the United States is busy with "operational programs" calculated to ferment the yeast of rising expectations. (See Chapter 5.)

Ernest Hemingway put it more succinctly when he observed that "what you win in Boston, you lose in Brooklyn." But diplomats, unlike baseball players, play *all* their games away from home.

Thus the host government, especially if it is an Emerging Nation, may suddenly wake up to find its treasury cupboard bare and demand of the Ambassador an X-million-dollar credit, to be available to the Minister of Finance by the following Wednesday. Or the State Department, prodded by an eager American representative at United Nations, may suddenly cable the Ambassador, directing him to twist the arm of the host government until the latter agrees to vote *yes* on some pending General Assembly item, even though the subject may have no more than marginal importance in the relations between the United States and the Ambassador's host country.

These events occur on weekends, when the Ambassador had planned to go fishing, or to catch up on his sleep, or to visit a hinterland province.

In the case of instructions dispatched by Washington, there is little awareness outside the geographic Bureau of the State Department of the mechanics of compliance abroad. There is no picture in the minds of other Potomac officials of the steps that have to be taken by an Embassy on the receipt of a message. Having dictated the phrase "you will accordingly seek an immediate interview with the Minister for Foreign Affairs, requesting an assurance on behalf of his Government that . . ." the task of the Washington bureaucrat is accomplished. He can then go home to his martinis, his backgammon, or his P.T.A. meeting, giving no further thought to the problem generated by his telegram until the Ambassador's reply reaches his Foggy Bottom cubicle.

But except in countries heavily dependent for survival on American bounty, and hence readily accessible to the American representative, getting an "immediate interview" with the head of the Foreign Office can be as difficult as it would be for the Washington representative of the country concerned to see on equally short notice the Secretary of State of the United States—even if the Secretary had not just flown off to attend a SEATO meeting in Canberra.

It may be revealing, therefore, to trace what happens to a message dispatched from Washington over the name of the senior member of the Cabinet, telling an Ambassador to take some kind of action.

The Embassy code clerk, having deciphered the telegram and having spotted the word "immediate," will have alerted the duty officer, noting the time—12:28 A.M.—in his log. But since the message is classified, the clerk will have been unable to describe its contents over the telephone; the duty officer, cursing, will accordingly read it in the code room at 1:30 A.M., as likewise recorded. Correctly refraining from waking up the Ambassador about something that cannot be tackled before daylight, the duty officer will appear at the Embassy Residence with the message at eight o'clock the following morning. He will be invited to share a cup of coffee with his Chief, who is already halfway through the local newspapers.

Most Foreign Offices do not open until ten in the morning, and the first question is whether the Ambassador should try to get through to a subordinate official before that hour, requesting an appointment with the Minister, or whether the Ambassador should make use of the Foreign Minister's private telephone number, communicating directly with him at home, notwithstanding the Minister's possible hostility to breakfast interruptions.

At that point there come into play factors that cannot be found in a rulebook: the Ambassador's assessment of the importance of the message, and its subject matter, in the scale of issues confronting the two countries. The Ambassador must weigh the message in terms of its impact on the host government. He will have to forecast the response of that government, and calculate how much of his own diplomatic ammunition is likely to be required, in order to produce the assurance demanded by Washington. He must decide whether—in the event that the cost in those terms may be considerable—the favorable reply of the foreign government is really an achievement commensurate with the expenditure of that much effort. (With Foggy Bottom bursting with bureaucrats, and all the bureaucrats supplied with paper, all sorts of messages reach foreign capitals demanding ambassadorial action.)

If he doubts the importance of the current project, the Ambassador can bounce back a message to Washington, setting forth his views and "requesting further instructions" —a gambit too frequent recourse to which can be irritating at home, especially if the majority of the Ambassadors receiving the same instruction act upon it without cavil.

In the case in point, the Ambassador concludes that an issue of substance is involved. The message deals with a proposed international conference on maritime jurisdiction, and the host country, possessing a seacoast and with appreciable fishery resources, should not only be interested in the project *per se*, but should be receptive to the views expressed by the United States. The Ambassador accordingly hunts up the Foreign Minister's unlisted phone number (given to him shortly after arrival, when the host government decided that the Ambassador knew his business). The Ambassador holds the receiver in one hand and his second cup of coffee in the other, while the Foreign Minister is wrapping a bath towel around his middle and pushing damp feet into bedroom slippers.

The Ambassador describes the situation set forth in the telegram, compressing it into its salient facts and expressing the belief that the interests of the two governments ought in this case to coincide. He bases the early approach to the minister on the unexpected United Nations action, scheduling with so little notice an Assembly debate on the issue.

After asking several pertinent questions, the Foreign Minister says on consideration that he agrees. He volunteers to cable his own UN representative in the sense desired, adding that he will tell his Ambassador in New York to get in touch with his American colleague. "No trouble, my friend. Your call has saved time for us both. I hope we can always settle our problems so quickly. . . ."

The Foreign Minister then returns to his bath. The American Ambassador, having scribbled his reply to Washington on a yellow pad, dismisses the duty officer and turns to the text of yesterday's White House press conference, received overnight in the Radio Bulletin. Mission accomplished.

The action described has taken place under optimum diplomatic conditions: a smoothly operating American Embassy Chancery with an efficient duty officer, an energetic Ambassador enjoying the confidence of the host Government and sharing a language with the Foreign Minister, and an issue soluble in terms of existing bilateral relations. Such conditions, in the troubled postwar period, are not always in conjunction. In Bolivia, Upper Volta, or Czechoslovakia, where interest in the law of the sea may be somewhat less than incendiary, the response will not be identical with that evoked in Japan, Great Britain, Peru, or Soviet Russia, even though all countries—landlocked or not—have the same vote in the General Assembly of United Nations.

Furthermore, leaving aside the variety of the responses toward the substantive issues raised by that particular message, the circumstances in which a reply is obtainable can differ even more widely, country by country and capital by capital. The Foreign Minister might be out of town, leaving a Vice Minister unwilling to commit his chief. Or, having been found within the inadequate time limit, the Foreign Minister might wish to consult his Chief of State, or his legislative leaders, and then disappear again, remaining inaccessible, until after the clock has run out. Or the host Government might be going through a period of annoyance with the United States, and hence decline on principle to cooperate. Or the American Ambassador might himself be out of town when the telegram arrives, with his Deputy unable within the prescribed period to reach an official of sufficient authority to handle the problem.

All of which is illustrative of the desirability of leaving diplomatic representatives long enough at their posts for them to learn how to operate effectively in the special and distinctive atmospheres prevailing in their respective countries. No two capitals are alike, least of all (for example) the five neighboring capitals of Central America, which share a common language and a common colonial heritage, but in no other particulars resemble each other.[2]

What American Embassies do have in common—in addition to identical stationery in the Chancery, a shared penchant for such double negatives as "it would not therefore appear inappropriate to observe . . .", and a persistent belief that "the Embassy feels" is a suitable euphemism for a straightforward "I believe"—is a pattern of organization. That pattern varies only in detail, whether the mission be in Asunción, Colombo, London, Tananarive, or Vienna. It

---

[2] It is gratifying to report that in contrast to the Roosevelt, Truman, and Eisenhower Administrations, which played musical chairs with American diplomats with such abandon that both furniture and participants were exhausted, and the business of American diplomacy suffered, the average length of ambassadorial service during the 1960s has almost doubled. This has been accompanied by a marked increase in the effectiveness of American representation at a number of capitals.

is the division of the mission into its component sections, and the manpower assigned to each; the "who does what to whom" of personnel operations overseas. That is as important to successful diplomatic operations as the arrangement of the orchestra is to a symphony conductor, whose counterpart abroad may well be the perspiring Ambassador, struggling to keep the woodwinds of his AID program or the tom-toms of his propaganda apparatus from drowning out his duet with the host Government.

The chart facing page 123 shows how an Embassy is organized. It is the product of a good deal of trial and error and of accumulated experience. But like all charts dealing with the human equation, it can only point the way; it cannot fuel the motor. The pattern alone is incapable of diplomatic performance. Like administration, organization is an adjunct to operations; it is not a substitute for the character or leadership of the Ambassador himself.

With that understanding, it should be worthwhile to consider some of the Embassy participants, including the Deputy Chief of Mission (DCM in diplomatic parlance), and the inhabitants of the Ambassador's "outer office." They play key roles in the success or failure of a diplomatic establishment.

The Deputy will be an officer with upwards of fifteen and often as many as twenty years of service at a succession of posts and under exacting conditions. He may be a man with the substantive rank of Minister in the Foreign Service, himself soon to be a candidate for appointment as Ambassador. In the most fruitful relationship with his Chief, the DCM will literally be the Ambassador's *alter ego*, sharing thoughts about all matters affecting the host country, in the same sort of partnership that ideally exists between a President and his Secretary of State. (Unlike the latter,

Standard Organization Chart
American Embassy Abroad

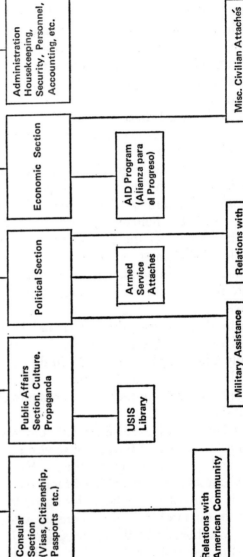

AMBASSADOR

Deputy Chief of Mission

- Consular Section (Visas, Citizenship, Passports etc.)
  - Relations with American Community
- Public Affairs Section, Culture, Propaganda
  - USIS Library
  - Military Assistance Advisory Group
- Political Section
  - Armed Service Attaches
  - Relations with Intelligence Community
- Economic Section
  - AID Program (Alianza para el Progreso)
- Administration Housekeeping, Security, Personnel, Accounting, etc.
- Misc. Civilian Attachés (Treasury, Agriculture, Minerals, Labor, etc.)

however, the Deputy becomes Chargé d'Affaires in the absence or incapacity of the Chief of Mission.)

In addition to acting as principal adviser, the DCM is also the operational head of the Chancery, responsible in the Ambassador's name for the smooth functioning of the entire diverse and unwieldy operation, from courtesy to the public in the issue of visas by the Consular Section, to suppressing beatnik tendencies in the Peace Corps; from having the Ambassador suitably represented at a rout staged by the local chapter of the American Legion, to seeing to it that a report demanded by Washington is not stymied because of the conflicting views of the Chief of the Economic Section and the Director of the AID program.

The DCM is the key individual in the Embassy, and he is also the hardest working individual in it, because the wise Ambassador will delegate to his assistant as much responsibility as he can, both to widen his Deputy's experience and to give the Ambassador more opportunity to deal with policy and with the problems of major significance. On the quality, diligence, and durability of the Deputy Chief of Mission much of the achievements of an Embassy will invariably depend.[3]

An Ambassador's "outer office," on the other hand, will be manned by personnel of junior grade, whose modest rank is not, however, a criterion of their usefulness or importance. On their handling of appointments and callers much of the public image of the Embassy will be formed, and on their direction of the flow of documents to and from the

---

[3] By the same token, a successful Ambassador is often known by the quality of the officers he trains. The outstanding American diplomat in that particular was undoubtedly Jefferson Caffery, who, during his long service as Chief of Mission, saw a score or more of his "graduates" become successful Ambassadors in their own right. From a single post—Habana in the 1930s—Caffery hatched six future Chiefs of Mission.

desk of the Ambassador and the DCM will depend the smoothness of the operation. One of the prerogatives of an Ambassador is the choice of his own secretary: good secretaries not infrequently attach themselves to a competent Chief of Mission, serving with him at successive posts, and by their knowledge of the chief and his personal ways of doing business, contributing substantially to the entire range of activities. A knowledgeable secretary, graduating to the title of "Special Assistant" and in charge of the "outer office," occupies a strategic spot, and she is only less valuable to the rest of the personnel of the mission than she is to the Ambassador himself. She should, incidentally, receive greater recognition in the Foreign Service hierarchy, and a more adequate salary.[4]

The Special Assistant is often in turn assisted by a junior Foreign Service officer, possessed of the language of the country, who handles reception of callers, pacifies those who have to be kept waiting, and acts as aide, protocol officer, and general expediter of business. An officer so placed automatically enjoys a unique view of the whole Embassy operation, receiving in the process exceptionally valuable training.

As the chart indicates, each Embassy is divided into five major components, of which the most important are the Political and Economic Sections, where the major part of the substantive work of a diplomatic mission is accomplished.

The Political Section is headed by a First Secretary, or in the larger missions by a Political Counselor or a Minister

---

[4] The author was blessed, across the years, by a succession of dedicated, competent, and personable secretarial assistants; his debt to them is hereby proclaimed, with gratitude and affection. Alas for diplomacy, most of them were mowed down by matrimony, with the Ambassador not infrequently giving the bride away, and his "outer office" thereafter chaotic.

Counselor for Political Affairs. That Section deals with the Foreign Office and with other Embassies, on levels appropriate to the officers of its staff. The Section also drafts diplomatic notes, develops relationships with political parties (including, in most countries, the opposition as well as the parties in power), and generally keeps tabs on the political life of the host country, about which the Section prepares reports, makes forecasts, and advises the Ambassador. It is the Political Section which usually maintains day-to-day liaison with the Defense Attachés and Military Missions, and with the intelligence community.

The Economic Section, which may also be headed by a Counselor or Minister Counselor, takes cognizance of practically all business that is not clearly political in character: trade, trade promotion, commercial relations with American business, dealings with Ministries other than the Foreign Office, financial matters including international loans and the foreign debt, and in general all matters relative to the economic development of the host country. Various civilian Attachés, including Treasury and Agricultural Attachés, serve as members of the Economic Section, which is also the Embassy's liaison with the activities conducted by the Agency for International Development (AID) and in Latin America by *Alianza para el Progreso*.[5]

The majority of the officers who serve as Deputy Chiefs of Mission, and later as Ambassadors, are graduates of the Political and Economic Sections.

Consular Sections of Embassies were until 1940 separate offices, in buildings apart from the Chancery. Traditionally

---

[5] In some countries, the Chief of the Economic Section simultaneously acts as Head of the AID mission, with personnel—depending on the size and scope of the program—that may run into hundreds of American and foreign employees.

the role of Consul has differed from that of diplomatic officers, in that Consuls dealt (and still do) with local officials, for which purpose the receiving state issues a special document called an *exequatur*, recognizing them and authorizing them to function. Moreover, until World War II, consular officers possessed fewer privileges and immunities than diplomats.[6]

The duties of Consuls cover a wide range of services to American citizens. The Consul General is usually the Embassy's principal point of contact with the resident American community. His Section is responsible for passport services, notarials, witnessing marriages performed in the country, and recording births and deaths of American citi-

---

[6] An incident occurring a generation ago in Buenos Aires illustrates this discrepancy. The wife of an American Vice Consul was soon to have a baby. Since Argentina claims jurisdiction over foreign Consuls in matters of citizenship of children born there, and is at times exigent about their liability for future military duty, the impending parents became preoccupied over the prospect that their son, visiting Argentina twenty years later with "Place of birth, Argentina" noted on his American passport, might be seized and thrown into the Argentine Army.

Two solutions were considered: to have the consular baby born on Avenida Alvear, in the American Embassy Residence, which was American, not Argentine, territory; or to have the Vice Consul commissioned as a diplomatic secretary, thus rendering him and his progeny immune from Argentine jurisdiction. The first solution not greatly appealing to the Ambassador's wife, who pointed out that there was no maternity ward in the mission, the Ambassador was prevailed upon to request Washington to issue a diplomatic commission, which was eventually forthcoming, but only after so much bureaucratic delay that notification thereof had to be sent to Buenos Aires by cable. The commission arrived one wing-beat ahead of the stork, which to the entertainment of everyone proceeded to present the young couple with a daughter.

For the past quarter-century, entering Foreign Service Officers are automatically issued both diplomatic and consular commissions, and the privileges-and-immunities distinction has largely disappeared.

zens. It also handles welfare-whereabouts-and-protection cases, including access to jailed Americans awaiting trial, plus miscellaneous services to tourists and travelers and on behalf of American vessels and seamen.

The most important service performed by the Consular Section for citizens of the host country is the issue of visas for those who wish to travel to the United States for business or pleasure, or as immigrants for permanent residence. In the case of certain countries of Europe that traditionally supply many future American citizens, the visa function alone may require a large staff and the maintenance of voluminous records.[7] Issuing visas is a Foreign Service function coveted from time to time by the Bureau of Immigration and Naturalization of the Department of Justice, which handles the entry of foreigners into the United States. Like so many other Washington agencies, the Department of Justice yearns to have a foreign service of its own.

Altogether there are one hundred and forty-six American consular offices scattered over the world, in addition to the Consular Sections existing in approximately one hundred and twenty Embassies established in capitals. The separate offices include sixty-eight Consulates General and seventy-eight Consulates: Canada, Mexico, and Brazil are the countries with the largest consular representation.

The Public Affairs Section and the Administrative Section complete the table of Embassy organization. They are relative newcomers to the diplomatic scene, dating from the end of World War II. The functions of the Public

---

[7] In 1960, one Consular Section in an American Embassy in Europe had 96,000 pending applications for immigration visas, or almost a twenty-year backlog against an annual quota of approximately five thousand. The pressure to obtain those coveted visas can well be imagined.

Affairs Section—public information about the United States, propaganda, and culture—were described in Chapter 6. The Section is headed by an officer of the United States Information Service (USIS), and it is noted from the Foreign Service List (publication of which was belatedly resumed in January 1967) that the titles of Press Attaché and Cultural Attaché are being superseded by Information Officer and Cultural Affairs Officer—one hopes with good results. It also appears that whereas certain countries are very liberally supplied with USIS personnel (thirty-three are listed in Japan, and twenty in Korea), little Kuwait is limited to one, and Gambia has none at all.

The tremendous postwar growth of the American Government abroad is reflected in the proliferation of personnel in successive Administrative Sections, which look after not only the housekeeping chores of the Foreign Service but likewise those of most of the other civilian agencies abroad. In Greece, for example, a country as popular with bureaucrats as it is with traveling Congressmen and American tourists, the staff of the Administrative Section of Embassy Athens numbers no less than *fifty* Americans, plus an even larger contingent of Greek clerks and assistants, as against a total of fifteen Americans in the Political and Economic Sections combined. That means that there are more than *three* administrators for each diplomat in Athens. The ratio in the African republic of Guinea (before most of the staff were declared *persona non grata* in 1966) was *eight* administrators against one officer each in the Political and Economic Sections.

The author defers to no one in his admiration for the tasks of diplomatic housekeeping well done, but the fact is inescapable that since the war no group has multiplied itself so persistently or in such abundance as have these teeming protagonists of the managerial revolution.

Along with this swelling of the ranks has come an almost equally impressive inflation of titles. That process began in Latin America during World War II, when Legations became Embassies and Ministers became Ambassadors; it was completed in 1967 with the promotion of the last two diplomatic missions—in Hungary and Rumania—to Embassy status. In addition to the one hundred and twenty Embassies now listed, there are nine Special Missions, headed by the United States Delegation to United Nations in New York City. That office alone is now larger than was the entire Department of State in Washington at the turn of the 20th century.

In this vast hierarchy, the titles of Vice Consul and Third Secretary of Embassy are in almost as imminent danger of extinction as the green sea turtle, the manatee, and the oryx. Not only does everyone want to play diplomacy, but practically everyone wants to be a Counselor of Embassy, a title which until a quarter-century ago was reserved for the Deputy Chief of Mission, but which has recently been employed to describe officials with scarcely more substantive duty than filling out requests for free entry of diplomatic supplies.

A culmination in this process was possibly reached in Vietnam by Ambassador (General) Maxwell Taylor, who took with him to Saigon a ranking officer of the Foreign Service to serve as Deputy Chief of Mission, with the title of Deputy Ambassador. Succeeding Taylor, Ambassador Lodge acquired *two* Deputy Ambassadors, plus a Deputy to a Deputy Ambassador—the last a Class One officer doubtless as busy as all the rest of them. Lodge's successor has continued the practice.

Having thus surveyed the composition of American Embassies abroad (those of foreign countries maintain but a fraction of the number of people sent overseas by the United

States), let us return to our nonexistent typical American mission. Its Chief began the day, as we have seen, by catching the Foreign Minister in his shower bath and inducing him to go along with the United States on an urgent United Nations maritime project. Let us examine how this particular diplomat spends the rest of the day so auspiciously inaugurated.

At nine-thirty the Ambassador reaches his Chancery, having walked the mile and a half from his Residence, to the disgust of the Embassy chauffeur, who can imagine nothing more idiotic than going on foot, when there is a Cadillac automobile to ride in. The first half-hour is spent reading the incoming telegrams, as well as the pink copies of messages dispatched in his name overnight, and in exchanging views with his Deputy, who congratulates the Ambassador on the expeditious disposal of the United Nations matter. Arriving half an hour before his Chief, the DCM will already have put the Chancery machinery in motion.

An informal ten o'clock meeting in the Ambassador's office will bring together the heads of the five sections, together with the DCM and the CIA representative. Here the day's work is considered, positions adopted, and assignments made. It is the most important meeting of each day, although once a week the Ambassador will have a larger staff meeting in the Conference Room—a sort of weekly summary and orientation session, a principal purpose of which is to tie all the members of the organization together, including Defense and civilian Attachés, newly arrived officers, and juniors getting their first view of how an Embassy functions.

Likewise once a week, the Ambassador will meet with his so-called Country Team, a diplomatic adjunct dear to the heart of Washington which invented it. The Country Team is not a voting organization, but a device to get before the Ambassador the views of the different agencies operating in the country, the progress they think they are making, and the problems they think they are encountering. Participants are encouraged to urge on the Ambassador any course of action they favor, and the Ambassador may or may not go along with those recommendations. When he does not, the matter can be referred to Washington: the subordinate's view, plus the dissenting opinion of the Chief of Mission.

A main objective of the Country Team mechanism is the hoped-for elimination of conflicting reports reaching Washington, a source of never-ending confusion during the 1950s, when non-diplomatic personnel dominated the scene and each agency was the architect of its own floor in the Tower of Babel.[8]

If the Ambassador has a speech to make, he will discuss it at his ten o'clock staff meeting, outlining what he thinks ought to be said, calling for comment, and then assigning to his Public Affairs Officer and to the Chief of the Political Section the responsibility of producing a "first draft" for further consideration. The more experienced the Ambassador, the fewer public speeches he will make, knowing that of the ills afflicting diplomacy, the most painful are those that result from an Ambassador's not keeping his mouth shut. On the other hand, he recognizes that an occasional appearance before a local Chamber of Commerce, and of course shortly after arrival at a new post before the American Society, can represent a useful opportunity to emphasize some pertinent truth or to get across some profit-

---

[8] In some of our larger Embassies, the Deputy Chief of Mission is chairman of all three of these Chancery meetings, thus leaving the Ambassador free to consort with the Prime Minister, to play golf with the heir apparent, and to brood about Larger Issues.

able idea about the work of the mission. Generally speaking, however, the Ambassador concludes that there are too many speeches and too many public statements made by officials abroad, just as there is too much vaporing in the United States by everyone from the President and the Secretary of State down to the smallest sub-cabinet member: the great uninhibited American penchant for sounding off.

The remainder of the Ambassador's morning will be taken up by appointments. At eleven he receives the Minister for Public Works, an evasive little man who has difficulty in coming to the point, which is the possible availability of credit to finance a dam and accompanying power grid; the Ambassador has present the Chief of the Economic Section and the Treasury Attaché. If the Minister will kindly submit a memorandum outlining the project, it will receive careful and sympathetic consideration.

Encouraged by this reception and impressed by the knowledgeability of the Treasury Attaché about his country's finances, the Minister for Public Works takes his departure, with the Ambassador as a mark of friendly respect accompanying his visitor to the elevator.

Then occurs the first untoward incident of the day. It involves the guardians of the Ambassador's outer office, which has been invaded by eight patriotic ladies from Texas, traveling together on a junket, and looking the part. Appearing at the Embassy without appointment but brandishing form letters furnished by their Congressmen, calling upon all comers to take notice, the ladies have been demanding to be received personally by the American Ambassador in order, so the spokeswoman declares, to bear witness.

The aforesaid guardians of the outer office, cognizant of their responsibility to protect the Chief of Mission from such hazards, have just completed a professional brush-off job, only to have it destroyed by the incautious and unexpected appearance in the hallway of the Ambassador himself, recognizable by the ladies even though he has a foreigner in tow and is not speaking English.

By the time the Ambassador is shaking hands with the Minister of Public Works, the eight ladies have surrounded the pair, while the spokeswoman leads her companions in rendering "Deep in the Heart of Texas" with sufficient volume to startle the jackrabbits into Mexico, if not to bring Sam Houston back from his Valhalla.

From the adjacent ambassadorial waiting room this scene is witnessed by the goggle-eyed Ambassador of Rwanda, whose eleven-thirty appointment to make a protocol visit to his American colleague is already twenty minutes past due.[9]

It takes the American Ambassador seven minutes to detach himself from the triumphant Lone Star ladies, and five additional minutes to explain to the bewildered and suspicious representative from Kigali what has happened. Meanwhile, the president of the American Chamber of Commerce, who heads an important American bank in the capital, and who has a twelve o'clock appointment with the Ambassador to discuss a piece of pending legislation which if enacted might adversely affect American interests, is in turn entertained by the Ambassador's secretary.

Having finally had his talk with the banker, at twelve-thirty the Ambassador, accompanied by the Deputy Chief of Mission, the First Secretary for Political Affairs, and the

---

[9] In diplomatic practice, a new Ambassador notifies all other Chiefs of Mission of his arrival; thereafter, as rapidly as may be, he calls by appointment upon each of his ambassadorial colleagues. In capitals having large representation, these calls consume much time and are often tedious for the busy American representative, who will, however, incur substantial ill-will unless he is accessible to the representative of even the most implausible nation.

Defense Attaché, in uniform, depart in the official limousine for the Peruvian Embassy, whose National Day it is. This consumes thirty-five minutes, which are by no means wasted. The Ambassador has a brief talk with the Foreign Minister, who shows him the text of the telegram dispatched to his UN delegate in New York, pursuant to their telephone conversation that morning, and then thanks the Ambassador for his courteous treatment of the Minister of Public Works an hour before—thus discreetly confirming the interest of the host Government in the Minister's dam-and-power project. The Defense Attaché picks up a useful crumb of information from his opposite Polish number, who has been mixing slivovitz with pisco sours and is feeling patriotic. The DCM and the First Secretary, who between them command five languages, cruise about among the guests, exchanging impressions.[10]

---

[10] Since World War II, and especially in the busier capitals, the interminable afternoon receptions to mark national holidays are being replaced by less costly and less painful twelve-to-one stag affairs, to which the foreign Ambassador invites officials of the host Government and members of the diplomatic corps, but not resident nationals, visiting compatriots, or members of the local society. This sensible arrangement results from the multiplication of countries and hence of national holidays. With as many as sixty or seventy separate countries represented in a single capital, officials would otherwise spend a disproportionate amount of their time rushing from party to party, congratulating each other on past revolutions.

Perhaps the next step may be for the host Government to encourage its diplomatic guests to join forces, on a monthly basis, and offer just one bang-up celebration every four weeks. Thus July, a month marked by a large number of national holidays, could witness a really rich and memorable affair, the cost shared among Canada, the United States, Venezuela, France, Belgium, Poland, and Peru, each of which could contribute according to its national specialty: truffles, champagne, bourbon, smoked ham, Caribbean crustaceans, pisco, and Canadian Club. The host Government, grateful to have seven celebrations compressed into one, with a

At one-ten, the DCM reminds his Chief that he is attending a luncheon at the Italian Embassy in honor of a visiting atomic scientist. They offer a ride to the Dutch Ambassador, and with the glass partition raised, they discuss for the next quarter of an hour various pending NATO matters, plus the latest news from Indonesia.

The Ambassador returns to his Residence at twenty minutes to four that afternoon. He is about to take a short nap prior to the arrival of the Economic Counselor and the head of the AID mission, to consider their unreconciled views on a long circular from Washington demanding a study in depth of the relative merits of economic versus military aid on the social structure of the country to which they are accredited, when the DCM telephones from the international airport whither he has rushed to meet an un-scheduled Senator, of whose pending arrival the mission has just been apprized by telephone from a neighboring capital. Although it is the height of the tourist season, a suite for the Senator has already been pried out of the leading hotel of the capital by the Administrative Officer. The DCM wants to know whether he should take on the visitor for the balance of the afternoon, or bring him to the Residence for cocktails, or invite him to dinner.

The Senator is not a member of the Foreign Relations

---

corresponding saving in wear-and-tear on its own officials, would gladly contribute the free use of the foyer and reception rooms of the National Opera, or even the turf and lavatory facilities of the National Stadium; all seven national flags could be displayed, and seven national anthems could be rendered in rotation, alphabetically.

An even better arrangement might be to have national receptions limited to six per year, continent by continent plus Oceania—except that this might possibly ignite a new Cold War among the congested participants.

(The views of the State Department on these laborsaving devices are awaited with interest.)

Committee. Insofar as the Ambassador and his Deputy are aware, he has no special interest in their country. The Ambassador suggests cocktails at the Residence at six-thirty, with the DCM to convey the Ambassador's greetings and to say he hopes to have a luncheon or a dinner in the Senator's honor, as soon as the Embassy knows the duration of his visit.

The Senator proves to be an affable guest. He leaves the Residence at a quarter to eight, three bourbons the richer and still chaperoned by the faithful Deputy Chief of Mission, and then the Ambassador sits down to a belated family supper, the first he has enjoyed alone with his family in nine evenings, after which he retires to his study with the papers that accumulated in his Chancery desk between his departure that noon for the Peruvian reception and the arrival of the Deputy, Senator in tow, six hours later. Having disposed of the papers, they are returned to the waiting duty officer, successor to the one who called that morning before breakfast, some fifteen hours before.

The Ambassador presently finds himself falling asleep over the latest issue of *Foreign Affairs,* whose writers seem to be getting farther and farther away from center, if not from reality. That night he dreams that eight determined women, wearing sombreros and boots, are punching his chest and pounding his stomach. The Ambassador wakes up, bathed in sweat. He takes a nembutal, and as he drifts off to sleep again, he concludes that somewhere, in some incarnation, there ought to be an easier way to earn a living. . . .

Part Two:
The Contemporary Scene

CHAPTER 9

Internationalism, Evangelism, and United Nations ⟨⟨⟨

THE PRECEDING CHAPTERS HAVE DEALT WITH THE AMERICAN foreign affairs apparatus, its organization, and the mechanics of its operation. It remains to examine how, in the years since World War II ended, the American Government has applied that machinery to the ingredients presented, bearing in mind that never before have those ingredients seemed so complex, nor more difficult of orderly mobilization. Many indeed continue to reach Washington red-hot, or else in leaky collapsible containers.

They are, nevertheless, the same ingredients that countries have always dealt with—ingredients derived from their national interests, real or imagined. The idea that modern democracy is confronted by something esoteric, or by new elements dating only from Hiroshima, is nonsense.

The largest collection of these ingredients in the world is housed in United Nations.

Down through the centuries, mankind has trodden a discernible path, often faint but never quite obliterated, searching for ways to settle disputes without recourse to war. Principles—markers of agreed-upon value—occasionally spot the way. Some were erected at Versailles in 1919, and others at San Francisco in 1945.

The 19th century, with its hundred years without major conflagration—Waterloo to the guns of August 1914—registered greater progress toward peaceful solution of problems than ever previously recorded. Improvement was especially encouraging in non-controversial and apolitical fields: the carrying of international mails, the extradition of criminals, the control of narcotics, patrolling the seas for icebergs, the International Red Cross, the regulation of fishing and hunting in various areas, the exchange of scientific and technical information. There were even advances in some of the more sensitive regions: suppression of the slave trade, arbitration of disputes, extension and use of good offices, the rules laid down in the Hague Conventions.

International law, simmering at the back of the stove since Grotius, in the 19th century had been cautiously edged closer to the burner. Humanity applauded.

And then, in 1914, the world exploded.

Amid the shambles of victory, President Wilson proposed an international organization, which the American people rejected. When other powers fell out among themselves, as they soon did, the League proved unable to settle their quarrels. In the short space of a dozen years, Italy and Japan, Nazi Germany and Franco Spain, all defied it. Mowed down by the guns of 1939, the League of Nations expired.

Nevertheless, the League was the first modern international organization that provided a continuously functioning machine established to deal with problems arising among states, including those of security and peace. The League profoundly influenced future developments. Its successor organization, born in 1945 in the closing days of World War II, bears many resemblances in form, in attributes, and in deficiencies to the short-lived League of Nations.

Like the League, United Nations has its Security Council, with its built-in veto in the hands of the permanent members. There is a General Assembly, with its one-state-one-vote rule. There is an international bureaucracy headed by the Secretary General. And once again there is the World Court. There are numerous subsidiary organs and agencies, of which the most vociferous is the Economic and Social Council, which is empowered to study, report, and recommend with respect to international "economic, social, cultural, educational, health, *and related matters*" [1] —as broad and tempting a warrant as could be imagined, and a standing invitation to evangelists to flex their fetishes. There is a Trusteeship Council, a World Health Organization, an International Labor Office, a Food and Agricultural Organization, and a host of other enterprises, most of them expensive and varying in usefulness.

The United Nations is thus a world organization, but it is not a world government.

Recognition of that all-important fact would avoid much needless confusion. United Nations is a league of sovereign states, theoretically founded "to maintain peace and security" and "to ensure . . . that armed force shall not be used, save in the common interest." (Mankind's old dream of peace, no less noble for remaining a dream. . . .)

But United Nations is not world government. As an institution it lacks sovereign attributes, including the power to tax, to raise troops, to pass laws; above all, UN lacks the power to impose its will. The weakness of United Nations, like the weakness of the League of Nations before it, is that is cannot compel obedience. Its mandates are

---

[1] Italics supplied.

resolutions or *recommendations,* but there are no teeth in them.

In becoming a member of United Nations, an individual state experiences no diminution of sovereignty. It merely declares that it subscribes to the purposes and objectives set forth in the Charter. To create a world government, each joining member would have to relinquish to United Nations a sufficient measure of its sovereign power so the total of the increments surrendered would be greater than the power remaining in any single state, or even any combination of states.

Such an establishment could (in theory) be the statesman's elixir, one potent drop replacing the jealousies and selfishness of the nations of the world by tolerance and a desire "to live together in peace with one another as good neighbors"—as it is written in the Charter. Another drop could produce a race of super-administrators, each of the highest competence and integrity. Whereupon thousands of drones now employed by Foreign Offices to complicate the issues could be pensioned off, tanks and helicopters could be melted down to make computers, and everyone would (in theory) live happily ever after. So say the evangelists of One World.

That large order does not seem likely to be filled in a predictable future. On the contrary, so accustomed are the separate states to forwarding their national, rather than their collective interests, and so dedicated are they to each individual territorial imperative, that promoting world government is left to the theoreticians and the evangelists aforesaid. Politicians want no part of it, and the statesmen among them prefer to take existing machinery, to keep it functioning, and to try to improve its performance.

To many, that seems a reasonable prescription. There is room for improvement. In dealing with substantive issues,

United Nations is effective today only when there is unanimity among the permanent members of the Security Council, which in practice has meant agreement between the United States and Soviet Russia, plus great-power willingness to join in collective action.

Since United Nations was founded, those two conditions have rarely been in conjunction.

The Security Council vote on Korea in 1950 is sometimes cited "to show what can be done," but that vote has little relevance for the reason that unanimity was achieved fortuitously—in the absence of the Soviet member, who had boycotted the meeting. Had he been present, he would have vetoed the proposition. Technically, the vote did produce a "United Nations mandate" establishing a crusade against (Communist) aggression. But in reality it did nothing of the sort. Soviet Russia denounced the operation as fraudulent, and then proceeded to undermine it. In fact, Russia was shortly abetted by the Red Chinese, who in November of 1950 sent half a million soldiers across the frozen Yalu River.

At Panmunjom, where the Korean armistice was signed thirty months after that, the "UN mandate" was buried.

Since United Nations was launched, political activity by the Security Council has been handicapped and at times paralyzed by the vetoes of the Soviet Union, which has utilized the Council not as a tool for building world peace, but as a propaganda platform. Rarely has Russia used United Nations political machinery for a constructive purpose. But notwithstanding American frustration over Communist tactics, the United States has not sought suppression of the veto. In present world circumstances, retention of its own veto power is clearly a matter of American prudence.

Thus the first task of American advocates of a veto-less

One World is to convince the American people that such a world would be a safe place to live in.

Along with the Security Council, the General Assembly has failed to measure up to the prayers of the framers of the Charter. They envisioned the Assembly as a sort of international parliament, where transcendent issues could be ventilated in resonant and reasonable debate; that debate in turn would be the final step in the formulation of World Opinion, before which a transgressor nation would tremble, and forthwith mend its ways.

Nothing of the kind has occurred. Censure by the General Assembly can be shrugged off, without penalty and even with nonchalance, and the reasons are not far to seek. Sanctions, unless the great powers themselves are in agreement, cannot effectively be applied to a culprit nation. And the one-state-one-vote provision, where the *No* of Ecuador equals the *Yes* of the United States, establishes an unsound foundation for political action—a foundation that has been further and perhaps irremediably shaken by the admission of all those tribal states, the gaudiness of whose regalia has been exceeded only by the irresponsibility of their spokesmen.

As a result, General Assembly proceedings have come to resemble more and more a police court in the Tower of Babel, and less and less humanity in congress assembled.

The judgments of the World Court have not seemed very much better. Some, in fact, have appeared to derive less from statute or sound judgment than from Alice in Wonderland or the operettas of Gilbert and Sullivan.[2]

That is not to say that the situation of United Nations is hopeless. For all its inability to define a collective will, and for all its failure to represent mankind's con-

[2] The asylum of Haya de la Torre, for example, or the status of former German South-West Africa.

science, United Nations is still a fruitful organization. Even when the Security Council bogs down in the permafrost of the Cold War, or the Secretary General makes a declaration unintelligible even in the idiom of his childhood, or the highest common factor of General Assembly operations seems to embody the lowest common denominator of futility, there are still positive things that a world organization can accomplish, that would not get done if United Nations were abandoned.

The most important of these is probably the habit of international collaboration, which is strengthened by the associations created by the mere fact of working together. Anything which fortifies that habit seems worth preserving both for its own sake and because now and then a political issue can be solved by first tidying up its nonpolitical components.

Again, although it is clear that one-nation-one-vote in the General Assembly ignores the realities of power, on the other hand, there is no reason why weak countries should not produce strong statesmen, nor why the latter should not make contributions to world affairs disproportionate to the resources behind them. Venizelos in World War I, Masaryk between the wars, and Hammarskjöld after World War II were not fettered because Greece, Czechoslovakia, or Sweden do not command vast armies. Today there is nothing to prevent the Foreign Minister of Iceland or Cyprus from being as eloquent or persuasive in debate as the representative of the Soviet Union or Brazil. In point of fact, weak countries throughout history have often produced strong spokesmen, because theirs is the greater incentive to do so. Lacking other resources, they can redress the balance by generating international figures, and even by producing an occasional statesman. A world organization fosters the development of international leaders.

Once more, leaving political dilemmas aside, there is a beckoning field for useful collaboration in the areas served by United Nations specialized agencies, as well as by the Economic and Social Council. There are tangible problems to be tackled and, notwithstanding over-emphasis on the value of the multilateral approach to them, many helpful operations can be undertaken. It is often less difficult to administer a remedy to an ailing society in the name of an international agency than as coming from a single country; for example, an insolvent debtor, seeking new credits to squander, may find the steps to be taken less repugnant if recommended by the World Bank than if outlined by the country it has importuned for further financing.

Lastly, although the world-forum aspect of United Nations continues to be exaggerated, nevertheless there is something, however tenuous or smudged, that is impressed on the momentary consciousness of mankind, or even transferred to the slate of history, by the actions of an international body dealing with an international issue.

Who can forget the Emperor of Ethiopia before the League of Nations thirty years ago in Geneva, after the rape of his country by Mussolini? Who can forget angry Portugal, calling upon the world to witness the seizure of Gôa by Nehru, that consecrated apostle of nonviolence whose credibility was forever after impaired? Who can forget Israel, hot with victory, rejecting before the General Assembly that new Soviet definition of aggression—namely, that aggression automatically occurs when a country armed by Communist Russia is defeated by a country armed with non-Communist weapons?

Who, for that matter, can forget the proclamation of the United Nations more than two decades ago at San Francisco, when for the battered world a better day seemed to be dawning?

Those markings on history's slate cannot easily be erased, and they are there because a world organization existed. The present situation, precarious though it may be in many dangerous particulars, would hardly be improved by abandoning United Nations.

United Nations owes much to the United States—perhaps too much for its own good. A worse headquarters than New York City could scarcely be imagined. Furthermore, a one-third contribution from a single member is not a healthy situation for the United States or for the other one hundred and twenty-two subscribers, whose casual attitude toward financing is heightened by riding on Uncle Sam's coattails.

Psychiatrists might possibly attribute American zeal for United Nations to over-compensation, or to recognition of guilt derived from denial of the old League of Nations. Having rejected the League, the pendulum of enthusiasm for United Nations was pushed too far in the opposite direction, over-compensation being an American trait, and evangelism an American weakness.[3]

At the outset, United Nations was thus too greatly sold to the American public who, expecting manna on the international platter, frequently found unappetizing the

---

[3] Evangelism is what befalls national self-interest, when self-interest succumbs to the Crusading Spirit. In foreign affairs, evangelism obscures clear vision. The notion that unhousebroken societies have a right to be industrialized at the expense of the American people is a manifestation of evangelism. So is the Peace Corps, much of *Alianza para el Progreso*, and the belief that warts can be removed from the body politic by recourse to United Nations.

As a steerage passenger on the Ship of State, evangelism may now and then be entitled to deck space, but it should never be allowed on the bridge in bad weather. And it should certainly not be mistaken for diplomacy.

tapioca that came out of the pantry. The American Government still contributes to this by appointing as its own
chief butler in the United Nations pantry a prominent political figure. The purpose, aside from finding a job for the
political figure, is admittedly to increase the stature of
United Nations. But over-advertising and over-expectation
result, and those are components rarely conducive to dealing
successfully with sensitive international issues.

The United States Delegation to United Nations, including a phalanx of Ambassadors surrounding the Chief
Delegate, is technically an instrument of the State Department. The Delegation receives its guidance from the President and the Secretary of State via a special Bureau of the
State Department established for that purpose.[4] Its Chief
is now an Assistant Secretary of State for International Organizations Affairs, and his countless myrmidons, acolytes,
and magicians are busy from morning to night, trying to
cope with the growing volume of issues of every kind and
description with which United Nations and its subsidiary
agencies are seized.

In addition to crash programs and *ad hoc* situations, there
is the annual agenda of the General Assembly, an almost
interminable list of propositions, on each one of which the
United States dutifully tries to determine its position in
advance. These "position papers" are supplemented by
other papers describing "fall back positions" which, short
of the solutions regarded by the planners as ideal, are nevertheless situations they believe that the United States "could
live with"—which in practice the United States usually has
to.

For weeks these papers are batted back and forth between

---

[4] Alger Hiss, an evangelist on the wrong side, was the first head
of that Washington office.

Washington and New York, where at each end they are argued, dismembered, edited, re-edited, abandoned, restored, re-argued, and finally agreed upon as the official positions of the American Government. As the date for a General Assembly approaches, the tempo of these activities quickens.

Official positions are likewise communicated to American Embassies abroad, with instructions to line up support for favorite projects. Of these, the hardiest perennial is Keeping Red China Out of United Nations—an enterprise notably assisted by the behavior of Chairman Mao himself.[5]

It is difficult to keep American UN activities from complicating bilateral relations, and during a busy General Assembly session it is often impossible to do so. That is because there are so many issues, with so many officials working on them, that the machinery—even with practically instantaneous communications, or possibly because of it—inevitably grows unwieldy and cumbersome. And there is rarely enough time for consultation between Washington and New York on the one side, and the American Embassies concerned on the other.

Another complication is that an American UN Delegation is always hectored and sometimes manned by earnest individuals who develop vested interests in this or that item of business, whether it be putting the world on the metric system, reforming the calendar, or saving the green sea turtle from extinction. Those may be worthy purposes, but in the hands of enthusiasts who draft cables, they are not always kept in perspective. Thus the American Ambassador

---

[5] Keeping Red China out of United Nations has involved an annual expenditure of American effort which, if condensed for use elsewhere, would have been sufficient to transplant the entire UN apparatus from New York City to Tahiti, with enough left over to staff the premises with Gauguin's granddaughters.

to Saudi Slobodia, up to his eyebrows in complicated petroleum negotiations, is not soothed by receiving a red-hot
telegram demanding an immediate promise from the Emir
to vote the straight bird-watchers' ticket.

Abroad, American Ambassadors are constantly sent scurry-
ing about on such errands, chiefly because someone in New
York has a brain wave, or because the Bureau of United
Nations Affairs in the State Department has too easy access
to communications facilities.[6]

In New York City there is a deal of undignified arm-
twisting in preparation for Assembly votes that are crucial
primarily to the self-importance or the dedication of other
Delegates, whose draft Resolutions if adopted will soon be
forgotten. That sort of thing keeps a good many people in
a great state of activity, without doing much harm or
achieving much progress.

Then there is the United Nations activity which results
from Sudden World Crisis, and that is the most feverish
UN activity of all. Leaving aside more recent instances,
let us consider the Congo Crisis of 1960, a fairly typical
confrontation, which lasted from midsummer until the
overdue extermination several months later of a chieftain

---

[6] A sample situation was described in Chapter 8.

In the case of the green sea turtle, the American Ambassador to
Saudi Slobodia, instead of firing back the first retort that occurs
to him, sends a Second Secretary to importune an official of comparable rank in the air-conditioned Saudi Slobodian Foreign Office.
The American takes with him a copy of the *National Geographic
Magazine,* containing an article on the hazards confronting the
threatened sea turtle, an article impressively illustrated by photographs in color. The Second Secretary reminds his colleague that
two years ago the Emir accepted from the hands of a representative
of the *Geographic,* who was digging for fossils in Slobodian sands,
a gold certificate of life membership in the National Geographic
Society, on the strength of which the sovereign Government of
Saudi Slobodia agrees to support the turtle-saving Resolution. . . .

called Lumumba, who had delusions of Communist grandeur.[7]

Luckily for the West, Lumumba's luck ran out, but it was a spectacular performance while Lumumba lasted. By that time the United Nations record contained thousands of words, many of them lava-hot, but since free-world and Communist objectives in the Congo were irreconcilable, nothing constructive was accomplished, except perhaps to draw attention around the world to the existence of the problem.

That incident and other crises before and after, including the Near East Crisis of 1967, illustrate the validity of an observation advanced by Jean Monnet, the French proponent of European Union, who warned that you "cannot safely put real weight on any international body which is

---

[7] It may be recalled that Belgium, cajoled by allies who ought to have known better, reluctantly agreed to establish the Republic of the Congo, although as Liberation Day approached, it became increasingly clear that the inhabitants of that vast region (except perhaps in Katanga) were approximately as ready to accept the disciplines of self-government as the crocodiles in the Sankuru or the bush-cows along its bank.

The Republic was nevertheless proclaimed, whereat all hell broke loose, precisely as Belgium had predicted.

Into these troubled waters, visiting foreigners plunged with alacrity—Russians and Chinese and Albanians and apostles of Fidel Castro—and every visitor had a walkie-talkie wired to his UN headquarters. As chaos in Africa grew, along the East River in New York the decibels likewise mounted.

Lumumba cavorted hither and yon, denouncing the West and threatening the missionaries. Presently Russian airplanes began to appear, supplying Lumumba with weapons and with man-size cooking utensils. To counter this, United States planes were mobilized; they undertook to evacuate stranded traders, churchmen, and administrators. At United Nations, each side accused the other, and as voices rose in angry altercation, Paramount Chiefs began heading for New York; rejecting the caviar, but accepting the martinis, they called for the passenger list instead of the menu.

founded neither on the realities of power, nor upon true community of interest among the members."

United Nations is of course just such an organization, and therefore its failure to produce a solution should come as no surprise to unbiased students of the contemporary drama. By the same token, proposals seeking to base United States policy primarily on United Nations should be regarded as pernicious and dangerous.

A useful step in the opposite direction relates to the Chief United States Delegate to United Nations. He should clearly and unmistakably be subordinate to the Secretary of State in Washington, whose prestige is impaired by having a political personage in the driver's seat in New York, even if the personage refrains from free-wheeling in Central Park.[8]

The American people should cease expecting too much from United Nations. They could then be gratified to recognize what it can accomplish. They could then find ways to accomplish that better.

Internationalism, on which much American participation in United Nations can legitimately be based, should not be accompanied by an exaggerated belief in the efficacy of

---

[8] A recent instance illustrates this. A ranking State Department official telephoned the American Delegate to United Nations to consider pending business. After discussion, which was cordial, they agreed upon points to be made by the Delegate in a speech the next day. The conversation ended with a remark by the State Department official that by way of confirming the understanding "instructions will be telegraphed you this evening."

"Instructions, hell!" retorted the Chief Delegate. "You forget I have Cabinet rank."

An "instruction," in long-standing State Department parlance, is any message that goes to the field over the name of the Secretary of State, just as a "dispatch" is any message sent in reply. But to the political personage in New York, it was beneath his dignity to be "instructed" by the Department of State.

multilateral, as contrasted with bilateral, operations. Although a great many useful things can be done under the canopy of United Nations, other undertakings, including solution of most problems that result from the hostility of the Communist world toward the free world, are beyond the competence of an agency that lacks the attributes cited by Monnet—realities of power and true community of interest.

For these reasons, uncritical reliance on "world opinion" as formulated in United Nations is likewise perilous. The manufacture and distribution of packages bearing the label "world opinion" is a major activity of Communist propaganda, and United Nations is a principal outlet. That is consonant with Communist exploitation of the fact that irrational acceptance of "world opinion" is a distinguishing weakness of the naively righteous and the righteously naive, who in the United States seem attracted to internationalism like mice to a granary.

These matters are understood in the State Department and even by most of the United States Delegates, but they need constant reiteration to the American public, who are active and optimistic, and eager to get on with whatever business is pending. American participation in international endeavors should be rescued from make-believe, and from unwarranted hoping, as well as from folly.

For the rest, a great deal of constructive work takes place within the United Nations organization, just as it does in the unpublicized day-to-day operations of the Department of State in Washington. That brave display of over one hundred and twenty national flags on the rim of Manhattan may often be that, and little more; but no matter how meager or limited that residue is, it is the most that mankind has been able to generate in his quest for peace and security, and that little should not be jettisoned.

CHAPTER 10

Communism and the Cold War

THIS CHAPTER DEALS WITH THE TOTALITARIAN DESPOTISM OF
the Communists, and with the struggle between that despotism and the free world for the domination of the increasingly congested planet we live on. More specifically,
this chapter has to do with the United States and Communism, and with the development of the Cold War.

The simplest distinction between free and totalitarian
societies is that in the free world the state exists to serve
the people, whereas in the Communist world the situation
is reversed—the state is all-important and all-powerful, and
the individual exists to serve the state. Those who have
escaped from behind the Iron Curtain can testify that this
is not a theoretical distinction.

The key word in the Communist (totalitarian) state is
unity, an imposed unity that does not admit of freedom of
expression or choice for the individual, or of political liberty;
it is the unity of total conformity. In this graveyard of freedom, unity is the topsoil covering the dead.[1]

---

[1] "Total conformity and despotism labeled as unity, and the ensuing denial of peaceful coexistence," wrote an observer recently,
"are the principles of [Communist dogmatism]. Our principle is
different [and] belongs to all men ... [It] involves everything called

154

Beyond that, we are not here involved with ideology, except to note that the dismal interpretations of Marx and Engels have little relevance to the changed conditions of twelve decades after the publication of the Communist Manifesto. In any case, it was Lenin, long after Marx's death, who drafted the blueprint for social revolution, and it was Stalin, the 20th-century Ivan the Terrible, who consolidated Communist power, and who brought on the Cold War.[2]

The winner in World War II was Soviet Russia, which emerged as the greatest land power on earth. *Militarily* invincible (except for the atom bomb, which Russia soon possessed), *politically* Russia was clearly the winner. Nazi Germany was destroyed. Japan had capitulated, allowing Russia to erase the losses of 1903, and Russia's erstwhile allies (barring the United States) were bled white. The Baltic republics had been snuffed out, and the Eastern European satellites were occupied by the Red Army.

The monolithic character of Kremlin power at the end of World War II was unchallenged. Even in distant Yenan

---

democracy; the open society instead of the closed one; government by discussion in an assembly of freely elected representatives of the people; the right to dissent instead of conformity; equality within liberty; inalienable rights ... independent of the will of majorities or minorities. ...

"Because we conceive moderation and limitation and approve of diversity, there is no need for us to be fanatical crusaders for our principle ... [but] because they cannot conceive moderation and limitation, because for them diversity is evil, advocates of totalitarianism are ... bound to be aggressive, the only limit to their aggressiveness being their own strength and their opponents' strength. ..."

From Max Salvadori, Dwight Morrow Professor of History at Smith College, Northampton, Mass.; *Smith Alumnae Quarterly,* winter issue of 1966.

[2] Lenin died in 1924; Stalin in 1953.

where Mao Tse-tung and his "agrarian reformers" were preparing the conquest of China, no voice was raised in 1945 in contradiction of the master word as pronounced in Moscow.

That was Communist Russia at the moment of Allied victory, the Russia that President Roosevelt persuaded himself might join in the Grand Design for a peaceful international community. Rarely has collaboration been more ardently sought, or would have been more genuinely welcomed had it been forthcoming.

Instead, as soon as Nazi Germany was eliminated, Soviet Russia resumed its drive—interrupted by Hitler's attack in 1941—for expansion of power and domination of peoples. That drive featured violation of wartime engagements, entered into on the part of Russia's allies both generously and in good faith; suffocation of freedom from Riga to Sofia and from East Berlin to East Poland; the looting of Manchuria; and the fastening of a Communist claw on occupied Korea.

Communist ambitions would inevitably have divided the world into two camps, but Stalin accelerated the process. Moreover, Soviet foreign policy was accompanied at a succession of international meetings by behavior so offensive that within the short space of two years after victory, the Kremlin had driven Stalin's former allies into a defensive coalition against him—a coalition soon to be formalized in the NATO alliance.

Stalin was the architect of that uneasy and dangerous balance known as the Cold War.

Today, the divided world is still the main fact of international existence, and the Cold War is the expression of that division. The continuing Soviet power drive, now augmented by that of the Red Chinese, is its principal manifestation.

The Marshall Plan, the Truman Plan, the NATO and succeeding multilateral pacts, and the military assistance programs all have their origins in the apprehensions aroused by Soviet behavior following the war.

The doctrine of containment (1947) was a response by the United States to the same challenge.

For the world, the quarter-century that has elapsed since Hitler's death can be divided into three periods, the second and third of which overlap. First there was the Stalinist (or bipolar) period, from 1945 to about 1954, the year following Stalin's death. Then came the period of Peaceful Coexistence, which began with Stalin's successors. That period in turn has merged into the third, characterized by Dogmatic Disunity as between Peking and Moscow. These three periods—Stalinist, Peaceful Coexistence, and Dogmatic Disunity—are arbitrary, with the reservation that as long as the Cold War endures, and the world endures the Cold War, perspective may be handicapped but signposts are convenient.

During the Stalinist (or bipolar) period, the fear of atomic annihilation was uppermost in the minds of men. For a decade after World War II, the danger of armed confrontation between Soviet Russia and the United States appeared so great that weaker powers were immobilized in one camp or the other. That was the period of the Greek Communist war, of the Communist coup in Czechoslovakia, of the Berlin blockade and airlift, and of the war in Korea. It was a time when little countries perched on the fence, frightened by what they saw, and fearing worse to come.[3]

It was simultaneously a period of other important de-

---

[3] Exceptions were several small but valiant countries on the side of the United States from 1950 to 1953 in Korea.

velopments: Western Europe revived, politically and economically. Greece and Turkey were salvaged. Austria was neutralized. Iran was propped up. Pakistan and India were born (each snarling at the other).

By hook and by crook, Soviet Russia acquired the atom bomb.

The Berlin crisis of 1949 was a spectacular and heroic demonstration of the feasibility of supplying a huge city by airlift alone, but it was hardly a victory for the West, because the Soviet threat was not squarely faced. (The Berlin wall came thirteen years later).[4]

The Communists seized mainland China. Nationalist China was established on Taiwan. France was expelled from Southeast Asia. Indonesia veered to the left.

Japan, miraculously restored, became a partner with the West.

Lastly, the monolithic Communist wall was split asunder by Tito. In 1948, the Yugoslav Communist dictator broke with the Kremlin, and lived to tell the tale. The failure of Stalin to liquidate Tito, after pinning the scarlet H-for-Heretic on his tunic, and the consequent emergence of Tito as an independent Communist dictator, shook the Kremlin to its foundations. The dogmatic unity established by Lenin and made supreme by Stalin at a cost of millions of lives had endured for thirty years. Tito's successful defiance (from which Dogmatic Disunity has evolved) was a gigantic Communist setback.

The second period was ushered in by Khrushchev's Peaceful Coexistence, and it included the short-lived Spirit of

---

[4] The issue in 1949 was access to Berlin, as guaranteed by wartime agreement. The Allies lacked the hardihood to force the *Autobahn;* they turned to the airlift instead.

Camp David.[5] During that period, fear of imminent nuclear war receded, and neutralism emerged. Freedom of action on the part of uncommitted states was resumed. Some of them became "neutral on the Communist side," fearing Soviet Russia (or China) more than they feared the United States.

Peaceful coexistence, a Communist device, was created both to lull the apprehensions of the free world—Stalin's behavior having belatedly been recognized in Moscow as a prime factor in mobilizing the non-Communist world against the Soviet Union—and also to give the new team in the Kremlin, the post-Stalin survivors, a chance to recover from the surfeit of frozen things left over in Stalin's icebox.

Like most of Communist semantics, peaceful coexistence wears an ingenious tag. A plausible sound was intended to distract attention from the built-in bear trap. The proposition goes as follows:

Since atomic conflict with the United States would be suicidal, atomic conflict with the United States must be avoided. The prospect of nuclear war should be replaced by peaceful, or competitive, coexistence. Before the end of the era of peaceful coexistence, the superiority of Communism will become apparent, and Communism will triumph.

This is the "we will bury you" thesis, with the corpse dressed up for the funeral parlor.

Then comes the baited trap, the poisoned arrow at the archery contest. Peaceful coexistence, in the Communist definition, not only does not forbid but in fact encourages

---

[5] At Camp David, President Eisenhower's mountain retreat in the moonshine area of Maryland, the moon shone briefly (in 1959) on Khrushchev and Eisenhower coexisting. The Spirit of Camp David evaporated when a U-2 airplane, complete with pilot, was shot down in the middle of Russia.

"wars of national liberation." And a war of national liberation in the same Communist phrase book is any uprising engineered by Communists against the constituted authorities of a non-Communist country.

If Communist foreign policy is to be understood, it is essential to bear that definition in mind. Thus the Communist aggression against Korea in 1950, and the aggression against Vietnam which the United States is opposing today, are wars of national liberation. The Communist-inspired (or Communist-armed, or -financed, or -led) movements directed against the Philippines, Thailand, and Burma, and against Central Africa and Latin America, may be the beginnings of wars of national liberation in those areas.

Peaceful coexistence, thus defined, is but another version of the Communist motto: "What is mine is mine, but what is yours is negotiable." That derives in turn from "the end justifies the means"—a basic tenet of Communist philosophy.

As did the first period, the period of peaceful coexistence witnessed important collateral developments.

Sputnik was launched, and the space race began. The atoms-for-peace movement was paralleled by a frightening expansion of the atoms-for-war capability of other countries, soon to include China.

With the spawning of new nations, doubling in a decade the flags in United Nations Plaza, the Communists created and still feverishly exploit the anti-colonialism issue.

The Hungarian revolt of 1956 was quickly and ruthlessly crushed, but it was followed by the gradual growth of satellite political initiative and by the phenomenon of Albania, unkempt and defiant, acting as Balkan pleasure-boy for Peking. (This was dogmatic disunity, casting an early shadow.)

The Suez Crisis of 1956 ended with the rescue of a

doomed Egypt by American intervention—one of the most costly errors of postwar United States diplomacy.

Castro's Cuba became the first Communist citadel in the New World. It was followed (1962) by the Soviet missile confrontation with the United States, from which Russia retreated. That defeat, combined with his agricultural failures, led to Khrushchev's downfall. (Downfall-without-extermination was an indication of changing Russia.)

A frustrated de Gaulle started to undermine NATO.

By the early 1960s, Communist propaganda which bragged that Soviet production would within a decade surpass the United States quietly withered away. The period of Peaceful Coexistence had begun to merge into the period of Dogmatic Disunity. That period displays Mao Tse-tung —successor to Marx and Engels, Lenin and Stalin—Chairman Mao, as the self-elected repository of Communist truth. To emphasize truth, the air is rent with invective; epithets hitherto reserved for imperialist warmongers are now poured daily over the Kremlin deviationists. The monolith of Lenin and Stalin seems irremediably shattered. Within China—turmoil.

Meanwhile, Indonesia rejoins the free world.

War is intensified in Vietnam, with growing repercussions within the United States.

Russia, having rearmed Nasser, in 1967 goads Nasser into provoking Israel to attack. Russia then woos defeated Egypt and her Arab allies: the renewal of an age-old Russian quest for influence in the Near and Middle East.

In equatorial Africa, the unwisdom of trying to make 20th-century nations out of 10th-century tribesmen becomes tragically apparent. In these waters of discontent both Moscow and Peking go fishing, each apparently convinced that if one lure won't work, perhaps a gill net will; and if both devices fail, maybe a stick of dynamite would bring the fish to the surface.

The Dominican Republic erupts (1965). The United States says No, with Latin America silently applauding.

Next door in Cuba, Castro remains on the Kremlin payroll, but flirts with Red China, while plotting private wars in an uneager hemisphere.

An aging de Gaulle continues to undermine NATO.

Before attempting to discover who, if anyone, is ahead in this exhausting competition known as the Cold War, it remains to discuss the doctrine of containment, since that doctrine for the past twenty years has guided the United States in its relations with the Communist world.[6]

---

[6] The doctrine of containment was defined by George F. Kennan, who was a Foreign Service Officer from 1926 to 1953, and again from 1961 to 1963. In the interval and since his retirement, Kennan has been a member of The Institute for Advanced Study in Princeton, N.J., and has lectured and written extensively. A Russian-language scholar, Kennan was the first to head the Policy Planning Staff when that office was established in the State Department shortly after the war; he served as Ambassador in Moscow in 1952 and 1953, and in Belgrade from 1961 to 1963.

The set of views that came eventually to be known as the "doctrine of containment" was first formulated in a telegram sent by Kennan as Chargé d'Affaires in Moscow in February 1946, and later distributed by the State Department as a classified document to American Ambassadors abroad. The doctrine first appeared publicly in the magazine *Foreign Affairs*, XXV, No. 4, July 1947, under the title "The Sources of Soviet Conduct," the authorship attributed to "Mr. X," a cover which almost immediately became transparent.

For the adoption of Kennan's doctrine, the nation is indebted to Dean Acheson, the Under Secretary and later Secretary of State, and to President Truman.

A revealing anecdote about Kennan's telegram is told by a member of Secretary Byrnes's staff whose duty it was to reach the State

In essence, the containment theory is as follows:

Soviet power can be likened to a body of water, which fills every nook and cranny of a vast shoreline and seeks constantly to expand. It can, however, be "contained" by the application of power at a constantly changing series of points around the edge of the shoreline. This requires energy, adroitness, and steady nerves on the part of the free world.

In order for containment to succeed, the inherent weaknesses of Communism must also be exploited. (This is the free world's answer to charges that "Communism, being aggressive, always has the initiative.") The inherent weaknesses of Communism include the difficulties of succession [7] and the insistent demands of the Russian people for a better lot.

Department early every morning, to skim through the telegrams received overnight from American diplomatic missions, and to prepare a digest to be on the Secretary's desk on his arrival. That summary was the first document perused by the Secretary each morning, and great care plus considerable talent was exercised in its preparation. Of the scores of messages reaching the Secretary's office overnight, only a small proportion were mentioned at all, and of those, few rated more than a summary phrase or a sentence.

Kennan's telegram ran to several thousand words—four or five pages of single-spaced exposition. It was nevertheless immediately identified as of national importance, and it reached the Secretary's desk intact, with the following chit:

"Mr. Secretary:

This telegram from George Kennan in Moscow is not subject to condensation. You will wish to read it in full."

In the two decades since his now famous message, George Kennan's views on Soviet-American relations have continued to command widespread attention and respect. However, in a volume of memoirs published in October 1967, Kennan declares (somewhat ambiguously) that in 1946 and 1947 he was talking about political, rather than military, containment.

[7] In 1947, when that was published, Stalin was at the peak of his power.

With respect to succession, all dictatorships are vulnerable in that they do not carry within them the seeds of continuity. The post-dictator period is invariably one of tension, and often of weakness or disintegration.[8]

In connection with living standards, Kennan reasoned that those would slowly rise in Russia, and that to the extent that the Russian people succeeded in retaining for themselves a greater proportion of what they produced, they might become more resistant to Communist exploitation and more desirous of conserving their gains and of living at peace with the world. The character of Communist dictatorship might accordingly change, both for that reason and because the evangelical fervor of leadership often peters out in the second or third generation.

Notwithstanding these vulnerabilities that should assist containment, Kennan foresaw no assured or imminent victory for the free world. On the contrary, the Communists themselves remain convinced of the inevitability of *their* triumph, and with time believed to be in their favor, they do not have to be hurried. Thus, with neither side desiring nuclear war but with Communism consistently seeking expansion, Kennan concluded that neither stability nor genuine peace would prevail within a predictable future.[9]

---

[8] From Alexander the Great to Catherine the Great, and from Genghis Khan to Trujillo, history is replete with dictators whose successors either frittered away their patrimonies or fell out among themselves or proved incapable of holding together the inherited machinery of government. Kennan thus had centuries of precedent for believing that on Stalin's demise the Kremlin machinery would be powerfully affected.

(Leaving Communist despotism aside, the sterility of dictatorship is perhaps unfortunate, because for a substantial part of the world's population—those lacking the discipline required to make self-government function—a "benevolent dictatorship" may be as good a government as the people deserve.)

[9] It should be remembered that Kennan was addressing himself to the problems of *Soviet* conduct. When his essay appeared, Red China was still two years in the future.

The Cold War has lasted since 1945, and it still continues.

Let us conclude by considering "who's ahead."

1. Communism is an upside-down missionary movement, with a theology of its own and a set of pigeonholes for the answers. This appeals to segments of the intelligentsia, including those who aspire—many honestly—to remake society. "From each according to his ability, and to each according to his needs" has a utopian ring, beguiling to the unwary.

2. During the half-century since Lenin and his conspirators captured Russia in the name of proletarian revolution, Communism has shown greater aggressiveness and more consistent leadership than the free world.

3. Communism has also shown a ruthless efficiency in the application and retention of power, whenever it has acquired it.

4. The territorial gains since Lenin are no less impressive. Predatory Communism has yet to surrender a single acre.

5. Communism has shown itself capable of technological achievements.

6. All of which contributes to impressing the uncommitted with the idea that change is often synonymous with progress, and that since Communism demands change, Communism must champion progress. In an era when many peoples are dissatisfied with their lot, including most of the so-called emerging nations, this permits the Communists to put the stigma of "reactionary" and "defender of the status quo" on their enemies. ("Our side is for change, our side is for progress; your side is against change and progress, therefore your side is reactionary. Our side is the wave of the future.")

The foregoing catalogue, formidable though it is, loses much on closer inspection. There are the inherent vulnerabilities of Communism cited by Kennan: the hazards of succession that afflict all dictatorships, of whatever ideology; and the possible modification of a Communist regime, if the people are given a better share of the fruits of production. There are other factors.

1. The free world is not, of course, against change. The free world advocates *evolution*, a saner diet than worldwide *revolution*.

2. Where the people have had a free choice, Communism has never won. In no fair election has a country "gone Communist." [10]

3. Communists have never been good at operating the economy. Although they begin, once power has been seized, by nationalizing means of production—thus acquiring their capital structure free—the purloined machines always run less well under doctrinal planning than they did before the winds of socialism bent the factory chimneys.

Communists are especially incompetent about agriculture. They starved millions in Russia and China with their macabre experiments, and they may starve millions more in the future.[11]

4. In spite of aggressiveness and leadership within the

_____

[10] The closest was Czechoslovakia in 1946, with the Red Army still occupying half the country, and with resentment against the betrayal of Munich still fresh in the mind of the electorate. Nevertheless, nearly two thirds of those voting rejected Communism. Furthermore, the Communist coup d'état of 1948 was triggered by recognition on the part of the Communist minority that in the then impending next elections, the Communist showing of 1946 would be reduced.

[11] It is nevertheless an ironic fact that the United States has consistently underestimated the Soviet potential, including the Soviet technological capacity. A friendly feeling for the Russian people has persisted throughout, but that has been coupled with a derisive contempt for the alleged Communist inability to keep the elevators in operation. American complacency was correspondingly jolted by the first Soviet sputnik.

Kremlin, Soviet Russia has not proved itself to be a stead-fast friend or a dependable ally.[12] A reputation for selling protégés down the Volga is not an international asset.

5. The position of Moscow with respect to "wars of national liberation," which under the banner of peaceful coexistence must be encouraged, is equally ambiguous. Short of starting a nuclear war, which Soviet Russia wishes to avoid, brushfire wars and guerrilla operations, which in the Communist guidebook are undertaken as preludes to wars of national liberation, are difficult to control, and even more difficult effectively to support. Brushfires, in a wind, can readily get out of hand. And the farther off they are from Mother Russia (or Father China, or Brother Castro), the greater the difficulty.

6. Throughout the far-flung Communist empire itself—Russia, China, Cuba, the satellites—each of the commissars maintains himself by the apparatus of the police state, that is by totalitarian despotism. Fear and hatred are corrosive propellants; sooner or later, the motor is affected, or the power plant is modified or replaced.

7. The effects of Peking's declaration of ideological war on Moscow remain to be assessed. Thus far, Dogmatic Disunity has generated more anathema than grenades, but obviously the Communist camp has not been strengthened by the loud quarrel between its two principal protagonists. The free world can take a degree of comfort from that, and the West may be sagacious enough to collect foreign affairs dividends from it, as well. The non-Communist world can-

---

[12] Those supported by Soviet diplomacy and then abandoned include the all but forgotten Iranian separatists; Israel, which Russia helped found in 1948; Cuba, in the missile crisis; the Congo of Lumumba; and the Greek Communists of the late 1940s. Another, with candidate status, is possibly Nasser. Others disappeared altogether; they came back from the ride with the lady inside, and the smile on the face of the bear: Latvia, Estonia, and Lithuania.

CHAPTER 11

Colonialism and Emerging
Nations 🖙

ANOTHER PHENOMENON OF THE 20TH CENTURY IS THE DIS-
mantling of the colonial empires of the European powers
and the establishment of dozens of succession states occupying the real estate thus vacated. These states were glued
together during the past quarter-century from the dependencies of Great Britain, France, Holland, and Belgium.

This chapter deals with the results of that operation, including Communist efforts to capitalize upon it, while simultaneously building empires of their own.[1]

Much nonsense has been written about colonies, and the
effects of granting independence to them. Such unqualified
statements as "all colonies involve selfish exploitation of
defenseless people" and "every colonial people would benefit from independence" have turned out to be utopian eye-
wash or Communist propaganda. Nowhere have the flames

---

[1] Germany, a late entrant in the scramble for colonial territory,
and Turkey, Gladstone's "sick man of Europe," lost their colonies
in World War I. The same conflict liquidated the Austro-Hun-
garian Empire. In 1898 the United States ended Spain's long colonial dream. Mussolini's Italy bowed out in 1943.

Of all the imperial powers of 19th-century Europe, Portugal
alone remains in possession of a substantial acreage of dependent
territory—principally Angola and Mozambique, in Africa.

of foolishness been more assiduously fanned than in the United States, where the arson of the crusading spirit has been stoked by the racial issue and the desire of Washington to attract the Negro vote. (How else account for the hostility toward Rhodesia on the part of the United States, which ought to be the last country to criticize another's declaration of independence?)

Or take the statement that "the end of colonial status will guarantee freedom." Freedom for whom, to do what?

The record of Liberia is illuminating. It is an example that ought to have been identified as the handwriting on the African wall, long before Guinea and Ghana and Rwanda defaced it with their own graffiti.[2]

Granted that the original impulses that led to the establishment of dependencies may not have been altruistic, those initiatives should nevertheless be considered in the

---

[2] Independence was bestowed upon Liberia by the United States over a century ago (1847), and thereafter the freed slaves, who had adopted the motto "The love of liberty brought us here," set upon the native tribesmen of the Grain Coast, reducing them to the status of second-class citizens. By the late 1920s, when a rich rubber company appeared and real money for the first time began circulating in Liberia, the idea of the Good Life as envisaged by the Liberian aristocracy—the fifteen thousand descendants of the freed slaves aforesaid—was the life of the plantation owners of South Carolina and Georgia, in the last years before the War Between the States.

The fourth decade of the 20th century saw Liberia accused before the League of Nations of "practices analogous to slavery," and the highest officials of the republic were implicated. Liberia met these charges, not by producing evidence of innocence, but by adopting what has since become known as the Adam Clayton Powell formula.

"Yah, yah!" snarled Liberia. "They wouldn't have accused me if I had not been black." And that was sufficient, even in 1933, to bring the United States galloping to Liberia's rescue.

For the last twenty years Liberia has been known as Tubman Enterprises, Unlimited, in honor of her perpetual President.

light of the circumstances prevailing in the 16th to 19th centuries. Times have obviously changed. Certainly the British proved not insensible to the issues producing the American Revolution: they learned therefrom, and others did likewise. (Some of the other colonial powers, in the modest American view, had less promising human material to work with.)

From the early 20th century until the wholesale granting of independence soon after World War II, the "exploitation" of dependent peoples by the metropolitan powers consisted mainly of efforts, underwritten by those powers, to identify local leaders and to train them in the tasks and responsibilities of government.

A glance at the areas of Africa where this search for native talent occurred reveals that it was not outstandingly successful. In country after country the assets contributed by the "imperialist exploiters" were quickly dissipated by the indigenous beneficiaries. The latter moved into the mansions of the Governors General and set up shop there, pausing only to build a pipeline into the treasury, which was soon empty. Successive administrative machines presently stalled or broke down, and replacements were unavailable. Soon the tribesmen complained that they were worse off than they were on the great day of independence, when the imperial flag was replaced by the emblem of elephant grass, palm fronds, and freedom.

As African succession state after state followed this lugubrious pattern, the military took over, and dictatorship resulted. Thus the post-colonial picture, for those hoping to witness the growth of representative democracy, emphasized instead disillusionment and confusion. From southern Sahara to the northern boundary of Angola, Rhodesia, and Mozambique, the spectacle was uniform, and uniformly depressing. Even Nigeria—populous and potentially rich—

even Nigeria, billed by the optimists as the shining equatorial exception, was soon stumbling toward disintegration.

Elsewhere than in Africa—and even in *Mediterranean* in contrast to *equatorial* Africa—the record of the succession states showed greater promise.

India and Pakistan, with their civilizations as old as recorded history, are clearly not to be spoken of in the same breath as tropical Africa; nevertheless, their ability to adjust themselves to the problems of the waning 20th century remains to be demonstrated. Their main difficulties—relations with each other, and control of the population explosion before mass starvation overtakes them—have not been solved. Pakistan has shown more gumption in several respects than India. In the latter country the image of Ghandi remains untarnished, but that of garrulous neutralist Nehru was impaired by the discrepancy between his interminable preachments of nonviolence for others and India's violent seizure of Portuguese Gôa for herself.

Difficult but not unsurmountable problems of management and development face Burma, Malaysia, and the Philippine Republic. Their futures will undoubtedly be influenced, perhaps vitally, by the outcome of efforts, led by the United States, to turn back Communism in Vietnam.

Indonesia experienced a unique and protracted affliction in Sukarno, the first President of the former Dutch East Indies. During nearly two decades of his mismanagement, Indonesia was the ungrateful recipient of vast American largesse; in fact, Washington's appeasement of the 1950s culminated in presenting West Irian to Sukarno, who expressed his appreciation by burning down the USIS installation, attacking Malaysia, and then demanding the rest of the island of Papua.[3]

---

[3] On the face of it, bludgeoning the Netherlands into surrendering West Irian appears to have been a shameful episode in Ameri-

On the brink of being delivered by Sukarno to the Red Chinese, Indonesia was rescued by the generals, who are still trying to clean up the mess and fumigate the premises. At this writing, the prospects of Indonesia are improved.

Another area that ought to show promise includes the northern tier of African countries, from Morocco to the western frontier of Egypt. In much of this strip French culture fused profitably with that of the fierce tribes of the Sahara. Mediterranean Africa, unlike the primitive jurisdictions where the inhabitants possessed little conception of national identity, can now be regarded as reverting to independence, rather than experiencing independence for the first time. Moreover, Morocco, Algeria, Tunisia, and Libya have not been fettered by exhortations to establish representative democracy the day before yesterday.

Israel represents a special case. Founded in 1948 with the blessings of the United States *and* the Soviet Union,[4] Israel received gigantic infusions of capital from sympathizers in the United States. Making shrewd use of these resources, Israel wrought a miracle in the ancient Palestinian land— an area coveted by one tribe or another since the dawn of history. If, after defeating Egypt in a lightning six-day war, Israel can produce statesmanship to match her martial and material successes, the future of one of the most potent of the succession states should be assured.

Lastly there are the all-too-numerous polka-dot countries: specks and crumbs of geography like Malta and Cyprus and the Caribbean Islands, or terrestrial swamps like Guyana or

---

can diplomacy—unless, of course, the Dutch importuned the United States to do it, in which case the official record has been, to say the least, deficient.

[4] Soviet Russia has since transferred her affection to Israel's archenemy Egypt, and to Egypt's Arab allies, as noted in the preceding chapter.

Belize, the majority of which were British Crown Colonies
and hence already acquainted with justice and public order.
Some of them—the Bahamas, and Jamaica and even mid-
Atlantic Bermuda—with winter sunshine and an established
reputation for hospitality—ought to prosper in their independence, at least for such time as they resist the temptation to shoot the tourist goose that lays the golden dollar.
Others, like Belize (British Honduras) with limited resources, will require hard work and superior leadership to
survive.

Still another, Cyprus, has already managed to shake the
NATO alliance by embroiling its two eastern members—
Greece and Turkey.[5]

Few of the polka-dot countries can be said to have gained
much by becoming independent. Like Haiti and the Do-

---

[5] Cyprus, an island with built-in racial hatreds and a bent-axle
constitution, is likewise a prime example of the American crusading
spirit in dreamlike orbit with anti-colonialism. When in 1960
Cyprus became independent, American prudence should have coun-
seled encouraging the British, with their long experience in distilling the juice of the bitter lemon, to go on distilling it in Nicosia
—that is, to continue their role in the island.

Instead, the United States surged forward, AID practitioners
in the van, with a gaggle of propagandists overhead and a clutter of
Peace Corps Volunteers underfoot. So firmly was the overstuffed
American presence soon involved that when a short time later Greek
Cypriots resumed shooting at Turkish Cypriots (to the annoyance
of Ankara and Athens), it took tremendous and altogether disproportionate American efforts to lure United Nations into tidying
up the island and admonishing the presiding Archbishop, who
promptly shouted, "Foul!" and appealed to Moscow.

The future of independent Cyprus, if it has one, is possibly as
a tourist haven for the eastern Mediterranean, especially Israel.

Since the foregoing was written, Cyprus has erupted once more,
and the United States has again had hysterics. Two solutions are
privately offered: (1) Move United Nations to Nicosia, issue
weapons, and quarantine the island; or, (2) recruit frogmen to dive
under Cyprus, saw it off, and let the island sink. Possibly the two
solutions could be combined.

minican Republic, which ceased to be colonies more than a century ago, they illustrate an ancient dilemma: whether good government which is imposed is better (or worse) than bad self-government.[6]

It is thus a speculative and chancy business to generalize about post-colonial prospects. Over threescore countries and areas and tribesmen reaching so-called independence since 1945 are too diverse and their resources are too complex for ready reference or automatic classification.

Among the beneficiaries of *anti*-colonialism have been the Communists, who have developed into an art form the technique of flogging the dead horse of Western imperialism. Such slogans as "foreign domination of other peoples must be abolished" and "all peoples are entitled to immediate independence," coupled with false assertions about empires and dependent peoples, some invented by the Communists themselves and others filched from liberal incantations, have been brought through agitation and endless repetition to "Communist axiom" status—that is, untrue but enshrined in the hierarchical vocabulary.[7]

---

[6] Haiti and the Dominican Republic, unhappy partners in possession of Hispaniola, have shown the least capacity of any countries in the Latin American world. Their soil is rich, but their history is a tragic procession of revolutions, assassinations, political and economic bankruptcy, coups d'état, and dictators, of whom Trujillo was the most competent as well as the most bloody.

When United States forces have from time to time been dispatched to restore order (most recently in Santo Domingo in 1965), the Haitian and Dominican Governments temporarily lost a measure of their independence, but the *people* gained more freedom than they had possessed before the Marines got there—and vastly more than during the thirty-year rule of the Dominican tyrant known in his lifetime as the *Benefactor de la Patria*.

[7] "As is well-known," is an introductory phrase identifying a Communist untrue statement. "As is well-known, the bestial rape of the progressive workers of San Juan by degenerate Potomac ghouls

Communist exercises in anti-colonialism have two practical purposes, each in connection with Communist expansion. The first is to turn the men of Africa and Asia against the men of Western Europe and the United States. To accomplish that, whatever gratitude those citizens might feel toward the grantors of their independence (or supporters of their independence, as in the case of the United States) must be replaced by hatred for alleged exploitation preceding independence.

Hence all past grievances must be exhumed, refurbished, magnified, and proclaimed. Where no grievances existed, grievances must be invented. In the accompanying din of reiteration and recrimination, many citizens of former dependencies, already bewildered by the problems of freedom, can be brought to regard the former colonial powers as oppressors, to the profit of Communist "liberators."

A second objective, closely allied to the first, is to create in these weak new countries, inexperienced in self-government and often short on self-discipline, confusion, breakdown of authority, disrespect for the institutions of government, and eventually chaos—on the theory that turbulent political waters are areas of maximum Communist potential.

It is to the credit of many of these inexperienced people that they have identified Communist activity and rejected it. Others, however, have been impressed, especially when the campaigns of hatred against "Western imperialists headed by the arch-imperialist enemy, the United States," are accompanied by offers of tangible assistance—guns, power plants, or credits, items geared to the rising expecta-

---

forced them into the snakepit of colonialism, thus paralyzing their march toward socialist freedom" is a typical Communist report, complete with metaphor and adjective trouble, of free elections in Puerto Rico.

tions of tribesmen frustrated by discovering that independence did not automatically usher in the millennium.

Although Communist anti-colonialist operations have not been outstandingly successful, they have generated odium and distrust, thus rendering more difficult the burdensome tasks of self-government.

In all of this the Communists violently reject the imperialist label as attaching to themselves. To Communists, all imperialism and all colonialism are sinful, and only Communist nations are free from sin.[8]

In contrast to the Communists, the United States shows disinterested achievement on issues relating to colonies and succession states, but it is also a spotty record, marred by clumsy good intentions as well as by mistakes.

The rapid progress of the United States after its own revolution two centuries ago, and its subsequent development into a world power, undoubtedly influenced the American people into endorsing "independence for everyone" as a sovereign remedy for political ills, regardless of the origins of those affected, or the disparity of the circumstances prevailing in other jurisdictions.

Having itself emerged from the colonial egg, the United

---

[8] The Communist colonial record is in fact thoroughly discreditable. The three Baltic states were devoured by Soviet Russia in World War II, along with slices of Finland and Poland. As to the six so-called satellites—East Germany, Poland, Czechoslovakia, Hungary, Rumania, and Bulgaria, for twenty years after the war their serfdom to Moscow was apparent to every observer on the free side of the Iron Curtain. The garroting of liberty in Hungary in 1956 outraged the conscience of the non-Communist world.

Red China shows an identical bent—witness Tibet, Sinkiang, and Mongolia as colonial pawns to Peking, as well as Chinese imperialist probes and thrusts in other directions.

The Communists endeavor to sweep these pages of history under the rug, while standing poised to stamp on any hand that seeks to lift the edge of the carpet.

States viewed sympathetically the phenomena of incubation and hatching, even though the American colonial period from the Jamestown of 1607 to the Yorktown of 1781—a century and three quarters of preparation for independence —bore almost no relation to the forced incubation of candidates for mid-20th-century self-government. The lustiness of the American colonial chick was not duplicated by the political hatching machine of the 1950s.

The successful emergence of the Philippine Republic also played a part in formulating the United States attitude.[9] The American heart had been warmed, in the dark days between Bataan and final victory in the Pacific, by the way in which Filipinos made the American cause their own, and died for it.

Here, believed the United States, was the answer to colonialism as practiced by others: enlightened preparation for early independence.

In the 1950s the American experience elsewhere was almost equally encouraging. Congested Puerto Rico, free to choose statehood, independence, or continued tax-free association with the United States, elected to remain an American commonwealth, to the bafflement of the Communist camp. Alaska and Hawaii were on the road to statehood. On the handful of American Pacific islands, the emancipated Polynesians were uneasy, but few of them engaged in anything more seditious than black-market nylons, or shacking up with a sergeant. Cuba, minus the colonial Platt Amendment, had collaborated loyally with the Allies in World War II and was enjoying economic and financial stability—or so it seemed in the early 1950s.

By mid-century the United States, having no important territories of its own left to consider, was inclined toward

---

[9] Serious problems were soon to germinate in the Philippines, some indigenous and some imported, but few were apparent at the moment of independence.

self-righteousness and imagining it knew the colonial answers. In that comfortable posture it was easy for the United States to fall in with criticism—even Communist criticism —of nations still possessing colonial dependencies.

In short, the United States concluded that anti-colonialism was a Good Thing and, as an extrovert nation, the United States proceeded to do something about it.

An unedifying spectacle followed. Doing something included needling the British and heckling the French and chivvying the Dutch and wheedling the Belgians, none of whom thanked the United States for badgering them to get on with the business of decontaminating themselves of their colonial possessions.[10] Worse still, the United States abetted the premature birth of new African states with the meddlesome fervor of an ambulance-chasing midwife, and the public cuddling of those same unhygienic infants in the 1960s was equally undignified.

To the extent that American official pressure accelerated these follies, the United States must accept a share of the blame for the headaches that followed, as well as for the reluctance of European partners to join in new crusades confected in Washington.[11]

---

[10] For the former imperial powers, decolonization was a traumatic experience, from the effects of which Western Europe continues to suffer. The United States, having for two centuries been a nation forging ahead, finds it difficult to imagine the frustration, and the sadness, of waning power and declining world prestige. Political scientists, immersed in the rising expectations of former dependencies, might well accord sympathetic study to the effects on Great Britain, France, Holland, and Belgium of the disintegration of their empires; specifically, they might seek to calibrate the loss of Indochina and Algeria with the attitudes of General de Gaulle.

[11] It is a wry circumstance that only Portugal, the most backward country in Europe, had the hardihood to tell the sponsors of colonial independence to jump in the Atlantic. Only Portugal refused to exchange what is left of the empire of Vasco de Gama for two more seats in the General Assembly.

As the foregoing discussion implies, the future of the ex-dependencies is far from assured. The remaining question is what the free nations of the world, and especially the former holders of colonial territories, ought to do about the problem. It is easier to pose the query than it is to answer it.

The notion that there is some magic formula for determining whether a given people, or a given unit of geography with people attached, is or is not "ready for self-government" has proved suspect among statesmen, diplomats and political scientists alike.

Political maturity is an enigmatic intangible, the "X" of the equation, which when present spells promise, but which when absent can render the problems of independence insoluble. Thus, although for most people independence is a legitimate objective, conferring independence prematurely has been a dangerous error.

The variety of experience accumulated during only a quarter-century of new-country launchings may be too limited for generalized assumptions, but it nevertheless points to several interesting conclusions:

That once-flourishing civilizations restored to independence after a colonial experience have a better chance of making good than primitive tribal societies with tropical environments.

That happiness and well-being have not been *significantly* advanced by exchanging independent for colonial status. In a number of places they have clearly diminished; in others, including several "developed" ones, they have probably grown.[12]

That countries showing the least capacity for self-government will have the greatest difficulty in preserving their independence, but that the trend toward military dictator-

---

[12] This is offered on the assumption that agreement is possible on the definition of happiness and well-being.

ship in such countries strengthens their chances for survival. That may be another way of saying that democratic self-government is not always a success, and that a substantial segment of the human race appears to have little talent for it.

That a number of succession states will never be viable. They are the Bolivias of the Bongo Belt, condemned to scrabble at the bottom of the pyramid of society. They are not "emerging nations," but nations that may never emerge. They are the states that lack not only the "X" of political maturity, but likewise the "Y" of material resources. (In a competitive world the Have-Nots lack what the Haves have, not because they are brown or black, or yellow or white, but because they do not have what it takes to succeed.)

That in spite of historical example represented by city-states and other small political units, many of the 20th-century polka-dot countries are impractical and will not long survive.

The territorial omelets of the past quarter-century cannot be unmade; no egg can be put back in its shell. For better or for worse, the world is stuck with over seventy post-World War II nations, the majority of which used to be colonies or dependencies. Possibly a handful may turn out to be valuable members of international society. If a dozen are solvent a century hence, that might be cause for re-joicing. Some will stumble along, some will prosper, some will become congenital paupers. Some will be dictatorships, and some may throw out dictators. Some states will absorb others (thus renewing the debate on colonialism), and still others may elect to be absorbed.

The relationship with a former colony cannot be severed absolutely; some residue of culture, of commerce, of shared experience is bound to remain. That is fortunate, because complete withdrawal by Western powers would facilitate Communist penetration.

The Communists can be expected to continue to make trouble and to try to push the former colonies into the arena of the Cold War. Yet on their record, and especially on their colonial record, the Communists have unclean hands. It behooves the free world to keep lifting the rug under which the Communists sweep their leavings. In performing this act, the free world should point out that truth is surely an ingredient of peaceful coexistence.

It should also be recognized that the former dependencies are not owed a living by the rest of the world. The underdeveloped peoples have no inherent right to become developed at someone else's expense. The nations of the free world can assist, on mutually profitable or on onesidedly generous or even philanthropic terms, but they have no compulsion to do so.

Much has been written about obligations involving the "human concerns of human kind," the so-called Fourth Dimension of foreign policy. "Let us not rely solely on the traditional economic, political, and military elements," goes this exhortation. "There is also a Fourth Dimension of foreign policy—the human concerns of human kind."

Solely implies that until the recent discovery of the Fourth Dimension, statesmen were unaware of the relevance of compassion, tolerance, and benevolence in shaping foreign affairs. That is not so. No policy that ridicules the human concerns of human kind would be worthy of the heritage of the American people. Those matters nevertheless must be kept in perspective, and the Fourth Dimension, inflated out of all proportion in the twenty years since American aid revived Western Europe, should now go back to where it belongs.

It was Winston Churchill who wrote, long before the

attempted beatification of the Fourth Dimension: "In victory, magnanimity; in peace, good will."

That being so, perhaps the best legacy that the free world can convey to the states that used to be colonies is a knowledge of birth control, together with the ambition to use it.

CHAPTER 12

The Good Neighbors and the Diet of Ambivalence 🦅

GOOD RELATIONS BETWEEN THE UNITED STATES AND LATIN America must rest on true and solid foundations: recognition of responsibility for shared occupancy of the New World, and respect. More often than not, this task has proved too large for American statesmanship, which has tended to regard Latin America as peripheral in importance. Moreover, an atmosphere of make-believe has marred the relationship between the other republics and the United States, which went through the 19th century imagining that its own success was contagious, and the 20th finding out that it is not.

It is the thesis of this chapter that notwithstanding the divisive factor of *disparity*, which may continue to render the United States suspect among the Good Neighbors, it is to the advantage of each side to maintain good relations with the other.

Little can be done about the disparity between the United States, on one side, and the twenty Latin republics to the south,[1] except to bear constantly in mind that that factor exists, and that it affects every aspect of the relation-

---

[1] Plus Guyana (1966), the first new nation in South America since Bolívar, as well as various Caribbean islands.

ship. By culture, language, religion, race, history, resources, character of government, and power, Latin America differs from the United States, and the differences are enormous. Although the potential of several other republics—notably Brazil—is great, the power gap will not in this century be significantly narrowed.

Wealth amid poverty, and strength in the presence of weakness, are not happy combinations, nor are they conducive to good fellowship. The poor and weak inevitably envy the rich and powerful, and imagine the latter have designs upon them. That may be unfortunate, but since it cannot be changed, it should be accepted by the United States as one of the facts of New World life. Acceptance of it should dispose of the notion that the United States will be loved by the Neighbors; it will not be, and no more time should be wasted in Foggy Bottom dreaming up schemes to be popular or to gain affection.

Let us examine how the United States has comported itself toward the fundamentals of good relations in the hemisphere—shared tenancy of the New World, and respect.

The most important aspect of shared tenancy is *defense* of the environment, and there the record of the United States is good. It is much better than the American people are given credit for. The Monroe Doctrine (1823) protected the countries of Latin America in their defenseless years. Notwithstanding a faltering American course toward Castro's Cuba, it is still the best shield they possess, and it costs them nothing. That the Monroe Doctrine was effective at the beginning because of British support is neither here nor there. They were American troops on the Mexican border, at the end of the Civil War, who outfaced the French invaders and sealed the untidy fate of Maximilian at Querétaro in 1867; it was the United States that spoke for Venezuela in 1890; and it was the United States that freed Cuba from Spain in 1898.

A few decades ago it was fashionable to belittle American activities in the Caribbean and to deride the so-called Theodore Roosevelt corollary to the Monroe Doctrine, under which the United States moved on occasion to protect lives and restore order. Those moves were not always popular with the *caudillos* whose depredations were curtailed, nor with some of the politicians elsewhere in the hemisphere who believed—or who professed for local purposes to believe—that American interference with national misbehavior was reprehensible. Intervention, they called it, and did their best to make it an ugly word.

As perspective lengthens, the American record gains stature. Today historians remember that in no case did American forces remain on a Caribbean beach longer than it took to careen the leaking ship of state, to plug up the holes, and to render the vessel once again seaworthy. In each and every instance the adjacent premises were scoured and polished; an empty treasury was replenished; schools, hospitals, and roads were built; and local citizens were trained in administration. There was money in the till when the United States departed.

The Good Neighbor Policy was a timely reminder (1933) of Latin American sovereignty and of a growing sophistication on the part of some (not all) of the members. It was followed by the abrogation of the Platt Amendment, which seemed a better idea at the time (1934) than it did a quarter-century later, when Fidel Castro delivered Cuba to Communism.

The Good Neighbor Policy likewise facilitated acceptance at the Habana Conference in 1940 of the concept that "an attack on one is an attack on all," hailed by the propagandists of the era as the miracle that made the Monroe Doctrine multilateral—the policy of the continent instead of the United States alone. Not an impressive boast when set beside the realities of power in the New World, but the idea was nevertheless important when the United States itself was attacked at Pearl Harbor one year later.[2]

The sister republics seized upon the newly consecrated multilateral character of defense to point out to Washington that it would be difficult for them to repel extra-continental aggression with their bows and arrows—and therefore would the United States kindly supply tanks, rockets, and airplanes wherewith to hold an aggressor in check? The United States did so, and delivery of this martial hardware kept American military missions in business, at the same time promoting an arms race that contributed little to the defense of the continent.[3]

As for the buried Platt Amendment, mourners took heart from the Monroe Doctrine itself which, multilateral or not, has been twice unilaterally invoked in the present decade—in 1962 at the time of the Cuban missile crisis [4] with Soviet Russia, and in the Dominican Republic three years later.

By sending troops to Santo Domingo in 1965 the United States served timely notice that it is still in the hemisphere-defense business. That was an act of statesmanship and courage, even though the good effects were undermined by

---

[2] It may also be recalled that the same concept—"an attack on one is an attack on all"—became the backbone of the NATO alliance. See likewise Article 51 of the United Nations Charter.

[3] Maintaining a disposition favorable to the United States on the part of Latin American military leaders was none the less useful. The military in a number of instances are the best element in the country. Their esteem is worth preserving.

[4] It must be recalled, however, that President Kennedy failed to maintain the firm position first adopted in the missile crisis.

Washington failure to follow through, and by fuzzy diplomacy.[5]

The other republics showed a gratifying maturity of response toward the sending of American troops. A generation earlier, dispatching Marines would have created pandemonium in the hemisphere, with every *Yanqui*-baiter having hysterics. In 1965 there were only token objections, with various public critics observing privately that they welcomed the North American initiative; they agreed that one Castro in the Caribbean was enough. Furthermore, several republics consented to share with the United States the establishment of a peace-keeping operation, and they supplied contingents of their own troops for that purpose. This action, successfully concluded the next year, added a new dimension to the inter-American experience.

That the Dominican volcano is permanently damped is a

---

[5] The troops on arrival in Santo Domingo were ordered to sit on their hands. They should forthwith have disarmed the rioters, fumigated the subversives, and reestablished order. In a few days the city would have been tranquil. But in the event, weeks were wasted in sterile discussion, involving a handful of politicians and a scattering of armed trouble-makers ensconced in the central part of the capital.

At the same time, Washington made a shambles of its own diplomacy. A procession of special representatives and emissaries-without-portfolio were flown from Washington to Santo Domingo to harass the resident American Ambassador and impair his usefulness. They included the Ambassador's predecessor in office, the American Ambassador to the Organization of American States, an Under Secretary of State, and an Assistant Secretary, as well as agents from the White House itself. These supernumeraries converged on Hispaniola, set up shop in Santo Domingo, and proceeded to engage in separate, disparate, duplicating, and overlapping negotiations, all at the expense of the resident Ambassador, who either enjoyed the faith of his own Government or else did not. If he did not have the confidence of Washington, he should have been replaced; otherwise, he should have been supported by the President and his prestige maintained.

hope rather than an expectation, but precedents were set in 1965 that may be useful to the New World in the future.[6]

Meanwhile, the situation in Cuba tries American patience and is likely to continue to do so, at least until Castro is eliminated. Throwing Castro out is nevertheless a Cuban rather than an American responsibility.[7]

However, it is one thing to operate a hostile state in irritating, even dangerous, proximity to the United States, and another to export revolution to the other American republics. It is the primary responsibility of those Neighbors to counter Castro subversion and exterminate his guerrillas, but the United States should stand prepared to assist them if necessary. At the same time, it should be some satisfaction to Washington to recognize that Castro's unruly antics must often be as harassing to the Kremlin as they are to the United States, and that the cost of underwriting Castro's economic miscalculations can give little joy to the accountants in Moscow.

So much for hemisphere defense, in which American responsibilities have been discharged more often than not with credit.

Other American achievements within the area of shared responsibilities are less impressive, in considerable measure because of the failure of Washington to inscribe the word *disparity* in successive guidebooks. Often with the best intentions the United States has substituted *wishful thinking*, thus creating unrealizable hopes that have led to frustration.

---

[6] Next door in turbulent Haiti, conditions seem almost perpetually ripe for hemisphere action.

[7] The Bay of Pigs operation (1961) was a tragic experience for the Cubans who took part, but its failure was a fortunate (if mortifying) thing for the United States, which might otherwise have been saddled with indefinite occupation of the island.

Again and again the syndrome of the Brave New World has heated American blood, producing in Foggy Bottom a mystique in which the communicants believe that hemisphere occupancy results in shared purposes and ideals, noble in character and unlifting to the spirit. When fact clashes with this legend, the American people suffer hurt feelings.[8]

The hallucination of the Brave New World is a principal ingredient in speeches celebrating Pan American Day, where it is harmless enough: euphoria, with an axe to grind on the whetstone of the patriotic metaphor. It is when politicians demand that their constituents absorb this gaudy nonsense that pretense replaces perspective, make-believe dominates wisdom, and the outcome is gritty and uncomfortable.[9]

Worse still, when notions of this sort collide with the realities of disparity, they render unstable the American attitude toward the rest of the hemisphere. American policy veers back and forth: it switches from a too-eager fraternalism to the stern paternalism of the hard line. Thus the fraternalism of much of the 19th century preceded the severity of the (Theodore) Roosevelt Corollary, which prevailed during the first quarter of the present century. Then came the Good Neighbor Policy (1933), but that in turn was subverted by apostles who invaded Washington to celebrate the New Deal.[10]

---

[8] An early note of skepticism was struck by John Quincy Adams, a principal architect of the Monroe Doctrine, who perceived no great future for Latin America, and less for the survival in the other republics of democratic self-government.

[9] *E.g.*, President Kennedy's speech in March 1961, launching *Alianza para el Progreso.*

[10] That period, beginning about 1934, coincided with the American Guilt Complex: "We have sinned, Brethren of Latin America; we have intervened, Brethren. That was very, very wrong of us, but

The end of World War II saw Latin America sound financially (thanks to the North American policy of fair prices for their export products) but tired of austerity, and the ensuing spending spree left several republics bankrupt and a majority of the rest disgruntled. They wanted support, especially financial support, and they wanted it from Washington, on liberal terms. The Truman Administration was unimpressed, and that was followed by the hard line of Secretary Dulles and the early Eisenhower years. When that phase led to demonstrations against Vice President Nixon on a South American trip in 1957, the Potomac reaction was to go into reverse and scoop up Operation Pan America. That in turn became a Republican soft-line device originally suggested by the President of Brazil; it was purchased by the waning Eisenhower Administration and expropriated by President Kennedy, who gave it, in 1961, the *Alianza para el Progreso* label.[11]

Much of this switching and veering has been bewildering to the American people, and even more so to the Latin American tenants of the New (as distinct from the "Brave New") World. The Neighbors have enjoyed neither the hard nor the soft line; what they would really applaud is a

---

Brother Neighbors, we love you dearly." That was the era of Washington failure to defend American business abroad, with Cordell Hull grumbling that expropriation without compensation was naughty, but President (Franklin) Roosevelt waving his cigarette-holder. It was a period when United States policy toward Latin America was in danger of becoming a one-way street with an ever-shining green light for the rights of the other republics, but a dusty detour toward their obligations.

[11] On the basis of these experiences, a return to the malaise of the hard line should soon be in prospect—possibly when ingratitude for *Alianza*, coupled with criticism of North American meddling with Latin American domestic legislation, sours sufficient United States Congressmen to affect appropriations.

straight line, and that line adhered to. The Neighbors are
tired, in short, of the American diet of ambivalence.

To weigh the prospect that a straight line may eventually
be adopted by the Washington specialists in hemisphere
geometry, it is necessary to consider the second of the two
pillars on which good relations must rest—namely *respect*.
The Good Neighbor Policy [12] specified respect for *obligations* as well as respect for *rights*.

It is essential to understand that rights and obligations
form an inseparable pair; they are Siamese twins, and it is
not possible for one to survive without the other. Unless
rights are respected, weak states are in danger of losing
their identities and of becoming satellites or dependencies.
It is, nevertheless, as much the duty of the weak to fulfill
their obligations as it is for the strong to abide by theirs;
unless obligations are respected by both weak and strong,
the relationship between those of disparate power is likely
to be corrupted by *appeasement*.

The United States record in respecting the rights of its
neighbors is reasonably consistent and, on balance, good.
Its record in not requiring fulfillment of obligations on their
part—that is, the American record of *appeasement*—is deplorable. Time and again, and especially during the years
that have elapsed since the Good Neighbor Policy was
proclaimed, the United States has diminished its effectiveness and tarnished both its self-respect and the respect in
which it is held by others, by turning the other cheek
instead of facing up to a problem.

Frequently small or weak nations have been encouraged
to flout their obligations because of the reluctance of Washington to appear to be a bully, or because Washington

---

[12] Before being spooked by certain New Dealers and by the
Coordinator of Inter-American Affairs, later Republican Governor
of New York.

wanted to seem "above indignation." On other occasions more important Neighbors have been responsible for acts of American appeasement. Property rights have been the elements most often at issue.[13]

At stake in these and analogous cases was, however, something more fundamental than property, or the principle that "expropriation without adequate compensation is wrong," vastly important though that principle is. The most important effect was that American supineness during the (Franklin) Roosevelt years encouraged Latin American disrespect for *all* obligations, at enormous cost to American investors, as well as to the good name of the United States.

It would be gratifying to report that the American appeasement record has since improved, but that would be contrary to the record. The United States put up for one year with the depredations of Castro in Cuba, when the issue of the violation of American rights ought to have been faced within the first few weeks after Castro came to power. In Brazil, likewise in this decade, Washington allowed repeated violation of obligations by a demagogic anti-American executive who might still be abusing American rights, had he not been overthrown by the military authorities of his own country.

It is in the Isthmus of Panama, however, that the flower of United States appeasement has found the richest soil in which to flourish. Panamanian politicians covet the Panama Canal. They have schemed for years to get it. They have dreamed of little else but swindling the United States out

---

[13] For example, the failure of the American Government to react more vigorously toward the expropriation of the properties of American petroleum companies in Mexico in 1938 encouraged expropriators throughout the hemisphere. In fact, what saved American oil properties elsewhere was not so much fear of possible American action as the ineptitude of PEMEX, the boondoggle established by the Mexican Government to administer the purloined properties.

of the waterway, and of living in opulent indolence ever after. In their quest they have invented all manner of complaints and grievances against the United States. They have repeatedly vilified the American Government and people.[14]

Since 1915 the United States has operated the Panama Canal for the benefit of the commerce of the world, without prejudice or discrimination, and to the very great profit of the Republic of Panama. Few enterprises as creditable as the Panama Canal are inscribed in the ledgers of history. Nevertheless, Washington, across the years, has bribed the Panamanian politicians to desist from this or that poisonous behavior, by raising the Canal Zone ante, which stands today at *eight* times the originally stipulated rental.

Other modifications of the original treaty, favorable to Panama, have been accepted by the United States, but each modification has been pounced upon by Panama as "proof" of original American sin. What the *politicos* now allege is that leasing the jungle in the first place, together with the right to exercise control within it, was a shameful act on the part of the United States, for which reparation must be made.

In 1964, over an issue already settled in Panama's favor (flying the Panamanian flag), riots destroyed hundreds of thousands of dollars' worth of American property. This was deliberate and wanton destruction, incited and carried out within Panama, but instead of denouncing the perpetrators and demanding compensation as a condition precedent to discussion, Washington in effect declared: "If Panama will deign to reestablish diplomatic relations, the United States promises to reconsider the 1903 Treaty."

As a consequence of "reconsideration," the United States

---

[14] Addled American liberals, including those who ten years ago identified Fidel Castro as the Robin Hood of the Sierra Maestra, loudly endorse this nonsense.

now proposes to surrender control of the Canal Zone, with Panama henceforth to participate in tolls and administration—a sell-out of truly mastodon proportions.[15]

The other side of the appeasement coin is equally unattractive. It is the presumption of superiority, which from time to time manifests itself in a lofty and patronizing attitude on the part of the United States in its dealings with other countries. It is most often displayed in recognition of new Latin American governments—in practice, regimes established by coup d'état or violence, at whose birth the midwife of democratic procedure was not in attendance, and whose antecedents are accordingly suspect.

The United States views most extra-constitutional changes of power with surprising distaste, considering its own revolutionary origin, and Washington time and again feels impelled to try to do something about it. Groping for leverage, the State Department seeks to connect extension of recognition with a promise of future good behavior, or with a rebuke or an indication of disapproval of past dereliction. This is a chancy and delicate operation. Recognition is an attribute of sovereignty, and once extended, it cannot be revoked. If a Government changes its mind, it cannot

---

[15] Leaving aside the question of appeasement, who except the Panamanian *politicos*, dreaming larcenous dreams, assert that the existing treaty is archaic? Does anyone else allege that the present management is incompetent, or that it will be improved by inviting Panama to jiggle the elbow of those opening and closing the locks? Does anyone in his right mind believe that Nasser and Suez constitute a favorable recommendation?

And why foreclose American options on a second oceanic canal, should it soon be necessary to dig one? At least four other sites are under investigation, several outside the Republic of Panama, whose spokesmen, notwithstanding their histrionics, desire above all else not to lose the lucrative American presence. Why should the United States deliver itself into their hands? Appeasement is the only explanation.

"unrecognize" or "derecognize"; it can only break off relations, a step often identified in the public mind with dangerous possibilities. Those limitations should warn foreign
offices to tread warily, and to avoid striking artificial poses.

So long as the United States has operated within the established confines of the three standard criteria of recognition, it has been reasonably successful.[16] It is when the
American Government has presumed to add criteria of its
own—such as extracting a promise to hold early elections,
or to maintain some unpopular commitment of the over-
turned government—that official spokesmen have mounted
the high horse of presumption and gone clattering across
the stage to the accompaniment of boos from an unap-
preciative audience.

As in the case of appeasement, it would be pleasant to
record that Washington is at long last discarding its superior airs, but it would be difficult to reconcile that with
the facts of Potomac behavior. The official attitude toward
a recent change of government in Argentina is revealing.

First, Washington deliberately delayed extending recognition, on the publicly expressed grounds that it did not
condone the action of the Argentine military in removing
the previous executive from office. Thereby Washington
irritated not only the Argentine military, but all citizens of

---

[16] The three standard criteria for recognition are effective control
of the instrumentalities of government, absence of resistance to the
new regime, and professed intention to abide by international commitments. Washington is tempted to wander beyond these safe
limits precisely because its heart is pure—Washington is, in fact,
on the side of freedom, democracy, saving the constitution, and
clean international living. It is also tempted, because for the first
years of this century few Caribbean regimes could survive without
State Department approval. That is no longer true—witness Nicaragua in 1946 and Haiti in 1962—but the habit persists of seeking
to use recognition as a negotiable asset, with an American presumption of superiority spoiling the bargain.

that proud country, with no compensating gain for the United States. And secondly, when a few days later a visiting American professor was roughly handled by the Argentine police, the State Department did not limit its comment to the case in point (where reportedly there may have been ground for complaint). Instead, the American spokesman climbed into a Foggy Bottom pulpit, whence he launched at Argentina a sermon on the relations that ought to prevail between government and education.

An initiative in a different context, but equally patronizing and ill-bred, was undertaken in 1965 by a young United States Senator who traveled in Latin America. This volunteer emissary set out to explain to citizens and officials of successive South American countries the intricacies of North American hemisphere policy, thereby incidentally usurping the prerogative of the Executive. There was a comforting aside to the effect that wicked Wall Street no longer controls the District of Columbia.

The Neighbors were next told how to comport themselves in their domestic responsibilities. Their taxation habits received Senatorial scrutiny, as did the distribution and utilization of land in South America. The pecking order of *Alianza para el Progreso* was examined, and Africa was solemnly recommended as a suitable field for Latin American political activity.[17]

In a reverse situation, a foreigner who presumed to harangue United States audiences about civil rights, the slowness of desegregation, urban riots, or the inadequacy of American taxes, would be lucky if he escaped with his shirt on his back. He would almost certainly lose his *bombachas*.

It remains to consider *Alianza para el Progreso. Alianza*

---

[17] Only Fidel Castro appears to have adopted the Senator's African suggestion.

is the major United States effort in the 1960s in inter-American affairs, but it has not escaped either the blight of appeasement or the taint of the patronizing attitude.[18]

The *latinos* cheered the prospect of *Alianza* appropriations—here was a new gravy train, with a tunnel of love leading straight to the magic mountain—but they eyed the manipulation of their societies with reserve. To the extent that American conditions governing the use of *Alianza* dollars were relaxed (at Punta del Este, later in 1961), the Neighbors approved. But for the rest they were unconvinced and skeptical.

The Neighbors did succeed, however, in obtaining Washington acceptance of a prime piece of Latin American philosophy, long on their agenda, which they have made a part of their rationale of *Alianza*. Ever since World War II, Latin American leaders have agitated in favor of the theory that any American republic, simply by being underdeveloped, automatically is entitled to access to the Treasury of the United States, which should be obligated to supply credits for development purposes.[19]

---

[18] President Kennedy's official announcement of *Alianza* threatened to extend the welfare state to the Beagle Channel, ten thousand miles from the White House, where the Latin American members of the diplomatic corps had been assembled to help unveil the new revelation. It was explained that *Alianza* would hasten social evolution by encouraging legislation detrimental to the rich but beneficial to the poor. It was hinted that large American appropriations would stimulate these developments.

[19] Both the Truman and Eisenhower Administrations were incessantly importuned on this subject, without success until Vice President Nixon's trip to South America brought about an appeasing reappraisal.

The current theory is the Latin American equivalent of the dependent-peoples-are-owed-a-living program, discussed in connection with anti-colonialism. It is a theory universal adoption of which would be as disastrous to the solvency of the Haves as it would be pauperizing to the Have-Nots.

When *Alianza* still faltered and backfired, Washington's remedy was to increase still further the appropriations, and then, in 1967, to organize a Congregation of Presidents, in a South American country already so far sunk in the swamp of the mismanaged economy as to be almost beyond redemption.[20]

That is not, however, to say that everything *Alianza* touches has turned to ashes. In comparison with the claims made for it and the oratory expended upon it, dividends have not been overwhelming. Nevertheless, they have not been altogether lacking, and the benefits have been due in considerable measure to the competence of a group of *latinos* on the steering committee, and to the emphasis they have placed on economic integration, rather than on statism, socialism, and despoiling the solvent.

Economic integration, to be sure, is a more profitable slogan than has often attracted the attention of hemisphere leaders. It is high time that the idea takes root that the *political* boundaries left in Latin America as a part of the colonial heritage are not necessarily the best *economic* boundaries. The Central American common market is encouraging in that connection, and there are similar stirrings elsewhere. Economics, rather than sociology, may be an area where *Alianza para el Progreso* by mobilizing resources and focusing effort can operate with good prospects of success. There are other worthwhile fields to explore, including stabilization of raw material prices, family planning and population control, and conservation of resources.[21]

---

[20] This was a most elaborate and expensive barbecue—*un asado con cuero con presidentes*—which may go down in history as the perfect prototype of the kind of meeting that ought never in any circumstances to be held.

[21] *Alianza* should depend more in future on the talents, initiative, and growing experience of the Latin members, and less on raiding

Granting once more the immense power differentials that are involved in the inter-American relationship—not only between the United States and Latin America, but also among the Latin American states in relation to each other—the hemisphere system, as the century approaches its last quarter, shows encouraging strength and vitality. The complex of resolutions, treaties, declarations, and accumulated experience in living and working together as co-inhabitants of the New World is by no means all rhetoric and after-dinner speeches. It embodies wisdom and conscience, and it has scored impressive advances.

Mutual defense and the concept that an attack on one is an attack on all may yet be decisive in defeating the tactics of Communist subversion. In the pacific settlement of disputes, the hemisphere record is good. The Organization of American States can be a genuine instrument for ascertaining facts and for basing recommendations upon them; implementation of OAS suggestions can play an increasingly fruitful role in the future.

As for the United States itself, its Latin American experience has produced praise and blame, together with satisfactions and bruises. If a single conclusion is to be drawn from the events of the past few decades, it is that when the great North American partner produces a blueprint for hemisphere salvation, all hands had better repair to the nearest *cantina* for rest and recreation, but that whenever Washington acts without hesitation, responsive to an enlightened self-interest which also serves the general interest,

---

the American cashbox. Less ideology and more hard work would be welcome. Citizens of the United States by the same token of sobriety and humility should thrust aside the temptation to become intoxicated by the sound of their own advice-giving voices. They should remember that the habit of volunteering a moral judgment has not been one of Washington's most endearing characteristics.

then the respect of the inter-American shareholders is generally forthcoming. And respect, taking into account the differences that exist, is as much as the United States has a right to expect from its neighbors in Latin America.

CHAPTER 13

Push-Button Diplomacy — with a Prize for the Lucky Number

✦

DIPLOMACY IS THE CONDUCT OF OFFICIAL BUSINESS BY
trained personnel representing governments. The purpose
of diplomacy is to reach agreement within a framework of
policy; hence ambiguity is its bane, and precision is its goal.
But precision is not easy to come by, for although diplomacy is one of the oldest professions in the world, it still
lacks an adequate foundation of laws, or even of universally
accepted regulations. Diplomacy is therefore vulnerable to
the encroachments of eager outsiders, who want to play
games with it, and of undisciplined regimes that seek to
use bad behavior in diplomacy as a form of juvenile self-
assertion.

The United States has suffered on each of these counts,
but Washington itself is in considerable degree to blame.
A nation whose motto is "Anything you can do, I can do
better" has seen its authority in foreign lands undermined
by hordes of make-believe diplomats, numbering thousands
in some of the "underdeveloped" countries, who have
swarmed abroad in the execution of countless "action programs" the only connection of which with diplomacy is
that it may take diplomats a long time to repair the ravages
of some of their operations. The United States compounds

the congestion by seeking to clothe these multitudinous agents with the mantle of immunity, but it succeeds only in diluting the effectiveness of its professional diplomatic service and of increasing the difficulties under which it must work.[1]

Meanwhile, the badly behaved regimes, incited by elements hostile to the United States, continue to agitate against the conspicuous American presence. "Spontaneous" demonstrations occur. Mobs burn down libraries, overturn American automobiles, and sack official premises. Bands of rowdies manhandle American personnel and trample the American flag.

Even granting the premise that the United States presence in scores of countries is preposterously swollen, these vicious and irresponsible manifestations are far more serious than has been officially conceded. They demand much more determined action than the American Government has thus far taken.

---

[1] Foreign Governments would not put up with these invasions were they not tied to soft loans, free food, or other forms of largesse devised by the aid program bureaucracy.

Even so, during the Arab-Israeli crisis of 1967, several Arab countries falsely accused the United States of aiding the enemy. When hatred swept like a sandstorm across the desert, American propagandists dropped their megaphones and dowsers abandoned their divining rods, and in compounds, post exchanges, and commissaries, the air-conditioning units stopped humming. For their salvation, hordes of employees of the United States, with their dependents and teachers and baby sitters, were hastily evacuated from the danger zones in the Near East to such havens as Athens, Istanbul, and Teheran, where they were given special allowances to tide them over "until the dust settled."

Most of these people, again at vast expense, have since been flown back to resume their chores among the defeated and resentful Arab populations—there to remain until the next explosion, followed by the next exodus.

They are serious not only because American personnel are endangered and the flag insulted, but because violation of diplomatic protection strikes at the root of international relations. They are serious not because diplomats as individuals merit special treatment, but because diplomats as representatives of a sovereign state cannot function usefully (and often cannot function at all) unless they are outside the jurisdiction of the receiving state, with their immunities from such jurisdiction scrupulously protected. Diplomatic immunity is not the luxury of a privileged class, but an essential ingredient of official performance.

Unless accredited diplomats receive the protection of the host country, a foundation of international relations is destroyed. It is as simple and as fundamental as that.

The remedy is unhesitating, decisive retaliation, together with a readiness—unless reparation is made and assurance regarding future conduct is received—to penalize an offending regime by breaking relations with it. The United States should forthwith consult with other Governments for the purpose of reestablishing respect for diplomatic personnel and premises, and of adopting a more forceful attitude toward violators.[2]

Successive Washington Administrations have shirked their duties with regard to this issue. Washington has repeatedly condoned reprehensible behavior because an emerging nation has yet to learn the cost of national delinquency, or because the United States ought to be too magnanimous to take offense, or even because a strong stand might jeopardize continuation of an aid program.

Respect for the American diplomatic establishment

---

[2] In this, the attitude of Soviet Russia will be of interest. Russian Communists, having developed during the past half-century the use of misbehavior as an adjunct to diplomacy, may now be as desirous as the West to see the trend reversed.

abroad is an item still dangling from the Foggy Bottom agenda. Forthright action is long overdue.[3]

In search of precepts that might provide a firmer foundation for the transaction of foreign business, and hence for the practice of diplomacy itself, the professors have recently been more active than the Washington hierarchy. The professors have evolved an ingenious assortment of rules, orders, and admonitions that are by no means without value in the conduct of international relations, even though a conclusion often reached by those engaged in diplomacy is that the difficulty of pinning down the imponderables reduces the effectiveness of guidelines. Furthermore, al-

---

[3] An issue in the bad behavior category involved the author nearly twenty years ago. Information had reached the Embassy that the host Government, bent on heckling non-Communist diplomats, planned to restrict the movement of the American Ambassador and his staff to points within a radius of fifteen miles of the capital; a restriction which, to say the least, would have complicated our operations. Accordingly, I called on the Foreign Minister, a surly type with a reputation for baiting the West, and I told him that if in fact his Government proposed to impose such a measure, it might be useful for the Comrade Commissars to know in advance that an identical regulation, applying to *his* diplomats in the United States, would be issued in Washington on the same day.

The threat was a sufficient deterrent. It was vastly more important for the Foreign Minister's diplomats to have the whole of the United States to roam around in than it was for the Minister to have the sterile satisfaction of keeping American diplomats within sight of Hradcany Castle. The Communists accordingly backed off, and the proposed restriction was dropped.

The point of the incident is that the expectation of prompt retaliation was sufficient to dampen the desire to misbehave.

As a postscript to the story, the Minister of Foreign Affairs might have been still more surly had he seen the message I had from Washington in reply to my report of the matter. By what authority, Washington wanted to know, had I threatened to anchor foreign diplomats to the District of Columbia? The American Government, said the message, was not geared to generalized surveillance of diplomatic representatives, and furthermore, it lacked facilities for enforcement.

though skull-practice and blackboard exercises may be useful in the diplomatic classroom, for a working diplomat to recognize when to ignore a precept may be as important as it is for him to memorize a congeries of political symptoms which theoretically ought to point in a given direction.[4]

These efforts to regiment the disorderly factors of volatile international situations—in effect, to computerize the uncomputerable—have nevertheless led to the erection of some handsome cairns along the diplomatic trail, over which perspiring statesmen, heavily laden with the responsibilities of office, should not necessarily stumble. A sampling might even encourage some of the climbers.

(a) *Turning the other cheek is poor diplomacy.* In individual relations, appeasement might seem an extension of Christian forbearance; moreover, "no one thought any the worse of Aeneas for letting Cerberus have his usual sop." [5] In international affairs, however, appeasement stores up trouble, and appeasing the weak is worse than appeasing the strong, first because it is unnecessary, and second because the weak are thereby encouraged to go on misbehaving. United States relations with former dependencies now experiencing precarious independence, as well as with some of the Latin American countries, illustrate the unwisdom

---

[4] A dean of the graduate school of this nickel-in-the-slot diplomacy is Professor Hans J. Morgenthau; those interested in the full treatment, including his "four fundamental rules" and his "five prerequisites of compromise" are referred to his textbook, *Politics Among Nations*, Third Edition (New York: Knopf, 1960). See likewise the views of Professor Schelling, mentioned in footnote 12 of Chapter 2.

[5] See Fowler's *Modern English Usage*, Second Edition (New York and Oxford: Oxford Univ., 1965), page 718 (under WORSENED WORDS).

of appeasing the weak. The case of Panama, where American appeasement has reached unprecedented heights, is mentioned in Chapter 12.

Appeasing the strong can sometimes buy time; for example, in September 1938, it bought one year of uneasy peace for Europe. Nevertheless, the tragedy of Munich—betrayal of Czechoslovakia apart—was not the time it bought, nor the fact that it settled nothing, but the euphoria it produced in the hearts of the appeasers.

(b) Another admonition involving the strong and the weak is that although in international affairs, *weak allies* can be useful, they *should not be in a position to commit the strong to a course of action.* That does not discredit the NATO alliance, which during the 1950s was a demonstration of weak partners growing strong behind the American shield. (The same can be said, less confidently, for some of the other multilateral pacts signed for protection against Communism.)

The blank check given by Imperial Germany to weak partner Austria-Hungary in July 1914 was cashed by the latter for World War I, with disastrous results. It can likewise be speculated that weak Axis partner Mussolini, by requiring Nazi assistance in the reckless Italian attempt to crush Greece in the spring of 1941, so set back the timetable of the Hitler attack on Soviet Russia that winter overtook the German armies before they could administer a knockout blow to Stalin. Had Hitler launched his attack on Soviet Russia in early May instead of late June, he might have reached the Kremlin.

The Korean war (1950-53) provides a more recent illustration. The United States listened to its weak allies (fifteen countries, furnishing three percent of the effort), and refrained from carrying the war to the Chinese Com-

munists in Manchuria, lest that bring in Soviet Russia.[6]
For opposing that decision, General MacArthur was dismissed, and an armistice representing not victory but a
stalemate was negotiated two years later. Again it can be
speculated that had the Korean war been pushed to a decision (as likewise advocated by the venerable President of
Korea), the even costlier American involvement in Vietnam
might have been avoided.

In these situations there is no reason to expect that the
judgment of a weak power is likely to be better (or worse)
than that of a strong power—except that for the latter the
stakes may be infinitely higher. To the perplexity of the
prophets, and the confusion of the professors, it all depends
on the circumstances and on the kind of decision that is
being considered.

(c) *A Crusading Spirit is Not a Foreign Policy.* That is
the precept which is most often violated by the United
States, no matter how often its fingers are painfully man-
gled. For a century after independence the American people, engrossed in the problems of internal development and
mindful of the warnings of President Washington, trod
circumspectly on the uncertain terrain of foreign affairs.
Dealings with the established powers were marked by prudence and careful attention. Not so in the 20th century!
For the last forty years, and increasingly since World War
II ended, wherever the crusader's flag is raised, there camps
the lusty and purposeful American, disdainful of restraint
and snorting at caution.

The American people, abetted by their politicians, for
a generation have been defining their actions in terms of
moral content, instead of weighing them in terms of the

---

[6] It now seems clear that Russia had no intention of entering the
Korean conflict.

interest of the United States. Aid and largesse for backward lands, anti-colonialism, acceleration of development of the underdeveloped, the revolution of rising expectations, universal literacy, eradication of the boll weevil—there may be elements of virtue and even of wisdom in each of them, but determination is handicapped by the doctrinal approach, or by the idea that this or that ought to be undertaken because it might be a good thing for a rich country to do, or that the duty of the United States lies in this or that direction.

Whenever Government spokesmen start talking like that, it is time to replace the spokesmen and to elect in their stead those who remember that the bloodiest encounters of history have resulted not so much from cupidity and evil intent as from Purpose Raised Aloft. Holy wars have invariably invoked the Crusading Spirit.

Thus it is that successive Secretaries of State should come to Foggy Bottom equipped with a backdrop that would automatically unfurl above the Secretarial desk. That backdrop should light with dazzling brilliance whenever the Secretary opens his mouth to emit a declaration, and a legend should be displayed above the head of the speaker.

The legend should read: A Crusading Spirit is Not a Foreign Policy.

(d) An equally fundamental proposition, this time endorsed by historians and academicians alike, is that *the purposes of foreign policy should be consonant with the true interests of the state* and *sufficient resources should be available to reach a proclaimed goal.* (How "true interests" can be ascertained is not yet in the guidebook.) That is a dual project easier said than accomplished, as the rise and fall of the Third Reich illustrate. So, on a more comprehensible scale, does the Arab provocation of Israel in 1967. And so, in a different context, does the painful American involvement in Vietnam demonstrate.

(e) A companion admonition is that *in diplomacy the Inevitable Should Be Exploited.* "There is a tide in the affairs of men" is an encouragement to such exploitation, and the expression "taking time by the forelock" contains the germ of the same idea, plus the optimistic notion that the progress of the glacier can sometimes be accelerated: that is to say that the inevitable can be nudged.

The success of this gambit depends on the correct identification of the inevitable, as well as on the ability to prod it, about neither of which are there reliable diplomatic road maps. Perhaps it is here that push-button diplomacy offers its greatest challenge—with a prize for the lucky number. At all events, the desire to command an audience while triumphantly proclaiming "I told you so" testifies to the popularity of the exercise and to the efforts of statesmen to be prescient after the event. In the world of sports, the Monday-morning quarterback will sympathize with their predicament.[7]

---

[7] An American representative in a Central American republic once solved the problem of exploiting the inevitable, and built up a considerable reputation in Washington in so doing. In the days before airplanes, there was a banana boat for the United States every Saturday, and each week it carried the diplomatic pouch, with the reports from the American Legation to the Department of State. It was the practice of the Minister to write all his reports on that Friday before that Saturday pouch-day, but now and then to backdate one of them, in which the Minister would predict that such or such a development would shortly occur.

That event having duly taken place, the Minister would prepare just before pouch-day a second dispatch, beginning approximately as follows:

"The Honorable the Secretary of State, Washington, D. C. Sir: With reference to the Legation's despatch No. 379 of April 20, 1926, in which it was predicted that the President would shortly appoint Dr. Gonzalo Calderón to be Minister for Foreign Affairs, I have the honor to report that Dr. Calderón last night assumed charge of the Foreign Office. The new Minister tells me that . . ."

(f) Another adage, of more practical diplomatic application, is *Always Be In with the Outs*. That is the diplomatic equivalent of not putting all of your eggs in the one basket of an existing foreign administration. Amateur statesmen, including lame-duck *politicos* rewarded with embassies, are often impressed by the blandishments of the leaders of the party in power, who do their utmost to maintain the belief that their status is permanent. When they succeed, the foreign representative—busy strengthening his ties with the existing regime—often neglects to cultivate the Outs, to the embarrassment of the mission when the Outs become the Ins.[8]

A change of government under constitutional procedure, following an orderly election, does not always create a serious problem for a foreign Ambassador. It can nevertheless be extraordinarily useful for a mission—London is no exception—to have at least one member of the staff whose principal responsibility is the cultivation of cordial relations with the Outs. If on the other hand the change of government results from political upheaval—coup d'état or revolution—and if the foreign representative has carelessly failed

---

The American Minister was careful not to over-exploit his private inevitable, and he was well on the way to oracle status in the southwest corner of the old State War Navy Building where Latin American matters were housed, when a junior colleague, his Caribbean exile ended and a European post in the offing, started an awkward rumor. By the time that carefree young man embarked for his new post, the Minister's inevitability balloon had suffered an irreparable puncture.

[8] War-weary Britain provided an illustration in 1945, two months after V-E Day, when the Churchill Government was unexpectedly voted out of office. A Labor Government succeeded. In the American Embassy in London there was a young Labor Attaché, widely versed in trade-union matters, but almost unknown to the rest of the staff. When the change-over took place, the Attaché was on a first-name basis with almost every member of the new British Cabinet, and in the confidence of all of them.

to be In with the Outs, his usefulness can be destroyed and his mission in effect terminated.[9]

Now times have changed again, but the problem of being In with the Outs continues to sit on the left hand of diplomacy, ready for mischief.

(g) *Something-for-something is good business*; it is equally good diplomacy. Nations, like individuals they represent, are inclined to calculate value in terms of effort spent on acquisition. What a nation obtains without effort, or free of charge, it accordingly is inclined to treat lightly. Few are so naive as to think that gratitude or friendship can be bought with aid programs or handouts, or that purchased goodwill would be worth having if it resulted. Nevertheless a beneficiary country ought to provide some reasonable *quid pro quo*, even if that something-for-something is limited to what the United States regards as efficient utilization of assistance, instead of waste and corruption.

A criticism of the aid programs difficult to escape is that

---

[9] Being In with the Outs in a dictatorship admittedly requires nimble diplomacy, because a dictator is usually suspicious of any relationship by a foreign representative with those who might overthrow him. There is no simple orchestration for that one, and the score must often be played by the diplomat by ear, one note at a time, with results that can easily become discordant. For instance, there was little excuse in the 1950s for the dismissal of a ranking officer of the American Embassy in Habana, merely to mollify the then Cuban President, who had complained that the officer was consorting with his political opponents. Conversely, the effectiveness of an Embassy in dealing with the Ins can be impaired by careless association with those dedicated to exterminating the Chief of State, even if he only imagines that is the case.

A simple solution occurred to an American company operating in Central America over half a century ago: the company as a matter of policy always had two or three of the more prominent Outs on its home office payroll in the United States (lawyers "advising on local legislation")—as well as half a dozen fairly prominent Ins, on its *cordillera* roster. But that became known as Dollar Diplomacy, and the New Deal took a poor view of it.

no minimum standard of behavior has ever been required of those benefiting from the American taxpayers' dollar. Over one hundred and thirty billions of these dollars have been spent in approximately one hundred countries during the last twenty years, without (since the end of the Marshall and Truman Plans) significant profit for the United States. In the name of peace, the United States has given military assistance to seventy-nine countries, including so many pairs of traditional enemies that several wars have been fought with American weapons. During this period the United States itself has fought one major war and is now fighting another. Many aid-recipient allies have either failed to help, or sent token forces, and several are aiding the enemy.

Public criticism by a beneficiary of United States policies is not here the issue. The skin of the American people is not that thin, nor is the United States trying to buy favorable votes in the General Assembly by subsidizing a voter. But when a foreign Government engages in sustained anti-American agitation, belittling American purposes in the world, misrepresenting American activities, or heaping abuse and indignity on the American flag, then it is time to call a halt. When a beneficiary country behaves indecently, the benefits should cease.

In scrutinizing the conduct of alleged allies whose right hands are pledged to participate with the United States in high and noble adventure, while the left hand throws rocks through Washington windows, the Congress has shown more solicitude for American interests than the Presidency or the Department of State. When the legislature has sought to intervene, successive administrations have been inclined to babble about "flexibility in the conduct of foreign affairs," while respect for the United States has dwindled, and the deficit has mounted.

With something-for-something as a motto, perhaps

CHAPTER 14

The Echo of the Voice of Experience ⟨symbol⟩

THE PROBLEMS FACING THE UNITED STATES IN VIETNAM FIT, perhaps too snugly, into one of the precepts discussed in the last chapter. Preventing the advance of Communism across Southeast Asia is clearly a critical target; containment in that area is "consonant with the true interests" of the United States.

Had the United States not acted, Vietnam would already have disappeared, with Laos and Cambodia swallowed in rapid succession thereafter. Indonesia or Thailand would have been next. Soon, in that vast area between India and the Philippines, Communism would have been imposed upon millions of people. To prevent that from happening is to the advantage of the United States, and opponents of the war in Vietnam should not be allowed to forget it.

It is in the other half of the precept that American troubles are concentrated. That part declares that in addition to the national interest being served, enough resources ought to be available to reach the proclaimed goal, in this case liquidating the Vietcong "war of national liberation." To keep Communist North Vietnam from taking over non-Communist South Vietnam is an intelligible objective. All of the collateral things that the United States is trying to

do in Vietnam—infusing adrenalin into the local administration, winning support of the villages and villagers, creating respect for free institutions, bolstering the economy—all
those are subordinate to the main business of blunting the
Communist spear and containing its outward thrust. Yet it
is in the area of "resources available to do the job" that
American difficulties accumulate. It is there that miscalculations have occurred, followed by the frustration of recognizing that notwithstanding the dispatch of half a million
American soldiers and an investment that approaches the
astronomical, the power of the United States in Vietnam
has still been insufficient.

The American election compounds Washington's problem, because unless the American electorate agrees that the
national interest demands success, new hands are likely to
be summoned to the Potomac plow, a prospect distasteful
to any existing Administration.[1]

The alternatives facing the United States in Vietnam
fall into three categories, with various shadings possible
between one and another. They have all three been hotly
debated. The United States could call off its operations and
go home, "leaving the problem to be solved by the Viet-
namese people themselves," as the proponents of this course

---

[1] With the precedent of Eisenhower's Korean initiative sixteen
years ago, the temptation of a Republican candidate to offer "to
get the boys out of the rice paddies" may be difficult to resist, even
though Eisenhower's visit to Asia following the 1952 election accomplished little, except to emphasize to the Communists that the
United States would settle for a draw (which was then falsely represented as "repelling Communist aggression").

As a contribution to the inhabitants-of-glass-houses-throwing-
stones department, it may be observed that the dishonesty of 1953
in describing the Korean armistice as "repelling Communist aggression" is the origin of the so-called "credibility gap" of which
the Republican survivors of 1953 have accused the Democratic
Johnson Administration in the 1960s.

proclaim. This would place South Vietnam at the mercy of the Communists, including non-Vietnamese Communists; it would lead to a bloodletting of major proportions. It would set in motion the events outlined at the beginning of this chapter, leading to Communist domination of Southeast Asia. The international prestige of the United States would plummet, along with American effectiveness in other spheres of international relations.

In spite of the agitation within the United States, few sensible people support this alternative.

Or the United States could make a prodigious effort (short of using nuclear weapons) to win a military victory. At home, call off the space race, postpone the Great Society, raise taxes, impose controls, and enforce austerity. Choose guns instead of butter, and with the guns invade North Vietnam, capture Hanoi, break the back of Communist resistance.

The second alternative, albeit more logical than the pullout prescription, also finds few prudent takers. There are cogent reasons against it, including reluctance to force Russia and China into resumed partnership, or to risk an American showdown with Russia alone, as well as lack of public enthusiasm for the austerity that an expanded involvement would entail.

That leaves the third alternative—a negotiated settlement, short of decisive military victory, but preserving South Vietnam (and her neighbors) as free world states. It is toward such a solution that Washington has been bending its efforts, with little initial success and with a deal of irresponsible domestic criticism. The fact that this is the only feasible solution does not make it an easy one. The Communists are dedicated and durable. Their tolerance of warfare is high; they can absorb harsh punishment; but they are not invincible.

The Communists should continue to be exposed to punishment. The idea that the United States should stop bombing North Vietnam "in order to create an atmosphere favorable to negotiation" runs counter to every lesson of Communist behavior. Communists negotiate when other tactics—in Vietnam infiltration, subversion, terrorism, and armed attack—fail, or become too costly, or grow too painful. Washington is correct in offering to stop bombing the North when the Communists stop infiltrating the South. In the meantime, the United States should continue to exploit the advantages deriving from superior technology, logistics, and mobility—in short, Washington's ability to inflict punishment on an aggressive Communist enemy.

The experience gained at such cost in the Korean war has been obscured by MacArthur's tinsel phrase about victory, and by the deception of describing the Korean armistice of 1953 as a free world triumph. A more accurate statement, attuned to post-World War II realities, would be that in the circumstances of the Cold War, settlements short of both victory and surrender may have to be accepted, if nuclear devastation is to be avoided. The Korean armistice can be defended within those terms of reference, even though from the point of view of the United States it would probably have been better to pay the extra cost of pounding the Communists back to the waist of the Korean peninsula, which would have created a more viable anti-Communist country. Equally important, it would have left little doubt which side was ahead, and it might have prevented our having to fight the Communists again in Asia, a decade later.

The error of the Korean war was not the dismissal of General MacArthur, whose behavior left President Truman no choice, but the calling off of his successor, General Ridgway, when the latter had mounted a successful campaign and once more had the Communists on the defensive. The enemy had no hesitation then about calling for negotiations. On that occasion, Ridgway should have been ordered to maintain the pressure. That would have permitted the United States to negotiate from strength, a matter of the highest importance in dealing with Communist opponents. Instead, heeding fainthearted allies and defeatists at home, the United States relaxed the pressure. That, rather than failure to bomb across the Yalu River, was the mistake in Korea.

When the Communists in Vietnam have been sufficiently battered, they too will call for negotiations, at which point the lesson of Korea can be restudied with profit.

The longer the Vietnam war goes on, the greater is the prospect that Soviet Russia will seek to precipitate elsewhere crises embarrassing to the United States. That is the "create a diversion" technique, at which the Communists have had abundant practice. When the facts are in, it may be that the Arab-Israeli conflict of 1967 had such an origin, with Russia—having armed Egypt—encouraging Nasser to bring on the fighting. In that event, Israel by her lightning campaign snatched out of the fire American chestnuts which assuredly might have been badly scorched if the military situation had been reversed, with the Arabs occupying parts of Israel.

The tasks of American statesmanship in the Near East have been enormously facilitated by Israeli successes, even though those were partial rather than complete,[2] and the

---

[2] Israel might, for example, have overrun the area between Suez and the Nile delta, and then notified the world that Israel was prepared to open the Suez Canal, without discrimination, to the vessels of all nations, in the way in which the United States operates the Panama Canal. If peace continues to elude the eager United Nations negotiators, such an offer might still have beguiling possibilities.

Arab states may soon be forced by economic if not political exigencies to reach an accommodation.

A solution recognizing Israel and guaranteeing Israeli passage through the Suez Canal and the Gulf of Aqaba, coupled with withdrawal from Arab territory, will require more forbearance than either side has yet shown. That would constitute a rebuff for Russia, rather than a victory for the United States, but it might create at least a short-term solution that would be better than the last twenty years of animosity and bitterness, exploitation of which has so engaged Soviet attention.

For the present, Israel is right in declining to evacuate occupied territory, since occupation is the leverage toward rendering the Arab states amenable to steps indispensable to even a short-term settlement. Would-be mediators seeking Israeli withdrawal first are playing Russia's game, or naive, or perhaps both.

A long-time solution may be a long time in coming, because it presupposes the growth of a willingness on each side to tolerate the other. In the Near East the United States objective is straightforward and uncomplicated. The American people wish to see Israel continue to prosper, but that does not imply lack of sympathy for the Arab peoples. Good relations with the latter are equally desirable, on grounds of self-interest and on grounds of respect for the heritage and potential of the inhabitants of the Arab world. There is nothing in this that would deny legitimate Russian needs in the area.

Having failed in 1967 in the Near East, it seems likely that Russia—unless faced with a crisis in bilateral relations with Communist China—may go on probing: in Africa and in the Near and Middle East, or once more in Latin America, or again against the NATO alliance. In foreign affairs, it is always easier to make trouble than it is to cure it.

Despite the American preoccupation over Vietnam, the Atlantic Alliance remains of paramount importance to the United States, and there is no reason to think that Washington is unaware of this. The prospect that a lasting European settlement may eventually be achieved rests primarily upon the Atlantic association, which is likewise the guarantor that the "processes of peaceful change" will not become paralyzed, or be swept away by the forces of revolution. The combined strength and the mutual confidence of the members of the Alliance still represent the most effective shield against Communist ambitions. Hence the Atlantic Alliance continues to be a principal Soviet target.[3]

The defection of de Gaulle is one of the sore spots of the Alliance capable of becoming inflamed, but it need not produce an incurable fever. The United States, together with a majority of the allies, has met the problem of de Gaulle with skill and patience. Unspectacular behavior is probably the only way to deal with a leader whose activities strike many Americans as irrational to the point of paranoia. At the least, the actions of de Gaulle toward British participation in the economy of Europe, as well as toward the Atlantic Alliance itself, have multiplied the opportunities for Kremlin-inspired mischief.

In three of the main international areas of concern to America—in Asia, in the Near East, and in the Atlantic community—it appears therefore that the United States is not doing as badly as its enemies might hope and expect, especially if they make the mistake of basing their assessment on the decibels of dissent registered on college campuses or in the columns of the American press. To be sure,

---

[3] A concise study of the status and prospects of NATO is contained in "The Atlantic Alliance—Unfinished Business," a 1967 publication of Senator Jackson's Subcommittee on National Security and International Operations. It is highly recommended.

CHAPTER 15

Atom Bomb versus Population Bomb, or Winner Take Nothing

THE PREOCCUPATIONS THAT OUGHT TO ENGAGE THE ATTENtion of the 20th century can be stated in two propositions, totaling only forty-eight words. First, mankind has multiplied the likelihood of self-extermination through warfare, without a compensating increase in the ability of human beings to live together in peace (the struggle with Communism emphasizes this); and second, mankind has multiplied mankind, to the point where population is outstripping the earth's resources.

Every other problem in the world today shrinks toward insignificance before these two dangers.

From prehistoric times until midway in the present millennium, warfare depended primarily on the strength and skill of the individual warrior, met at close quarters. Formations of soldiers, deployment of troops, logistics, and tactical dispositions were all important, and as more states and nations developed, there were often more and more men on a side, but it was still the single warrior with stone or club or mace or sword, pitting himself against an individual adversary, who determined the outcome. It was David who slew Goliath, and Achilles who disposed of Hector, down through Greek and Roman times to the Dark Ages and the

Crusades, and finally to the Age of Chivalry. Destructive though warfare was, and although entire local populations were at times sacrificed by the conquerors, the survival of mankind was not menaced by that kind of struggle.

Gunpowder and the longbow multiplied the menace. Gunpowder reached Europe about 1250 A.D., and its military potential developed slowly, along with the development of iron and steel. The longbow in the 14th century ended the Age of Chivalry by making it possible for the foot soldier to unhorse the knight. Each made possible *killing at a distance*—that was its revolutionary aspect. The nuclear bomb is merely the final step in slaughter from afar, the ultimate development in absentee destruction.

The extermination-of-the-race hazard of war is thus a recent phenomenon. Earlier combatants killed each other just as dead with javelins and rocks as the corpses incinerated at Hiroshima, but they killed each other a few at a time—comparatively speaking—instead of over fifty thousand at a time, from hundreds of miles away.

The concept of total war probably antedates Napoleon, but before the 19th century ended, the machine gun had doomed mass armies—even though it took World War I to prove it. The machine gun led to static trench warfare, which gave way to tanks as that war ground to a close. The same conflict saw the airplane in operation—first, fighters (combat between individuals, a brief reversion to the Age of Chivalry), and then bombers, which were initially used to attack military objectives. In World War II, as aircraft grew in size and bombs grew in power, bombers were employed first against industrial installations, then against cities, and finally against the civilian population.[1]

---

[1] As destructiveness kept pace with the industrial revolution, apprehensions likewise mounted. There were efforts during the latter part of the 19th century and until the eve of World War I to con-

In 1945, with the introduction of the atom bomb, the annihilation of the earth itself became a possibility. War had finally achieved a potential for universal extinction. (At this point, John Hersey's *Hiroshima* becomes required reading.)

The war won, the United States recoiled from the implications of total power that sole possession of the atom bomb conferred. The American people accepted world leadership, and tried to do their best with it, but they rejected total power. Instead, the United States offered to share its nuclear secrets: it offered to harness and control atomic power, but to outlaw nuclear warfare. That was a generous and far-sighted initiative, but while Stalin's negotiators talked, his scientists in Soviet Russia—aided by the Communist espionage apparatus—themselves perfected an atomic weapon. The American nuclear monopoly was broken less than five years after it began, and before agreement had been reached on the utilization of nuclear energy.

By an irrational quirk of political astigmatism, the multiplication of nuclear capability that marked the 1950s resulted in reduction of worldwide forebodings. Post-Stalin Russia, now ostensibly dedicated to peaceful coexistence, and prosperous United States, clearly not seeking new horizons to conquer, continued to glare at one another without affection, but they gave to the rest of the world the impression that neither giant wanted to unleash the awesome destructive power at his disposal. Before the deterrent that each possessed, the other nations of the world relaxed, al-

---

trol the peripheral hazards of war, and even to reduce them. Statesmen took advantage of the hundred years of peace that ended in 1914 to draft humanitarian regulations, to protect noncombatants and prisoners, and to strengthen the rights of neutrals. These were important gains, but except for efforts on behalf of prisoners, most of them were swept away by the bloody tornado of World War II.

though several of them—Communist China included—simultaneously set about gaining nuclear capability for themselves. India espoused neutralism. De Gaulle buried his head in radioactive sand. Others chirped and whistled to keep up their collective courage.

That is the situation today, nearly a quarter-century after the bombs that ended World War II and ushered in the age of nuclear obliteration.

The population bomb has a lengthier and more complex heritage. The implications of over-population were recognized by a theologian named Malthus, nearly a century and a half ago, but his warnings went largely unheeded, partly because there still seemed to be enough food to go around, and partly because some of his hypotheses were faulty. Until Malthus, however, few questioned the validity of the Biblical injunction to be fruitful and multiply. In nomadic and later in pastoral societies, population density was rarely a problem, although the ancients understood that land could not support a limitless number. Children were useful because they helped with the chores—the consensus being that children produced more than they ate—and because children grew up to be warriors and parents of warriors. As recently as a single generation ago, Mussolini and Hitler were exhorting their respective compatriots to redouble their philoprogenitive efforts; the fecund female was publicly honored, and prizes went to those with the largest families. Throughout recorded history, and until half a lifetime in the past, the balance between people and food was maintained not by man's perspicacity—far less by his prudence, planning, or restraint—but by the first three horsemen of the Apocalypse: war, pestilence, and famine. (The fourth horseman is death itself.)

Bubonic plague, carried by fleas from infected rats, decimated Athens in 430 B.C. and Rome a century and a half later. The Crusaders are credited with reintroducing the black death into Europe, where in the 14th century it killed over one hundred and fifty thousand people in London alone. Another scourge, louse-borne typhus, devastated Russia and the Balkans in World War I. A third, cholera, has taken incalculable tolls, especially in Asia.[2]

Like pestilence, famine since earliest times has reaped bountiful but grisly harvests. Failure of the food supply has resulted from weather deficiences, especially drought, and from insect pests like the locust. In many areas, including much of Asia and India, where a substantial part of the population is marginal in the best of years, the victims of hunger multiply whenever nature's cycle falls below the fragile normal yield. Disasters such as hurricanes, earthquakes, and volcanic eruptions add further uncertainties to the unstable pattern.

Beyond these so-called natural causes, not produced by the hand of man, there is the third horseman—war. Since war dislocates society by interfering with the production and distribution of food, as well as by destroying safeguards to public health, military operations have been followed throughout history by plague and hunger. The more protracted or all-embracing the struggle, the greater the mortality.

Such balance as the world has known was maintained until recent times not by man's restraint, but by repeated catastrophe. The three horsemen, flanked by a high death rate for children and a short life expectancy for adults, kept in check the eager fertility of the human race. Perhaps that

---

[2] See Professor Hans Zinsser's *Rats, Lice and History* for a fascinating study of the influence of pestilence on the development of man.

has not been the most efficient way to run humanity's railroad, but at least until the modern era there were few pile-ups from too many streetcars named Desire, all trying to crowd into the terminal together.

Early in the last century the Reverend Thomas Malthus sought to elucidate these mysteries, and his essays commanded widespread attention. In simplified form, Malthus held, first, that in finite space (that is, the earth), nothing can increase without limit; and second, that population unless checked grows in geometric progression, doubling about every twenty-five years, whereas food supplies increase arithmetically, which is not fast enough to keep up. Therefore, Malthus concluded, population will outdistance food, and starvation and misery will result. Malthus likewise assumed that restraint (other than the three horsemen) was the only way to check the growth of population and that the threat of suffering was the most effective way to induce restraint.

As is sometimes the case among philosophers (and even among diplomats), Malthus was both right and wrong. He could not have foreseen the tremendous burst of agricultural productivity, on the threshold of which he died in 1834. The fourteen decades since he wrote have witnessed almost the entire scientific and technological revolution, with everything from the ungainly monsters of mechanized harvesting to hydroponic vegetables and chicken coops with one hundred thousand computerized tenants in each. Thus, down through the years since Malthus, food supplies because of the ingenuity of man have approximately kept pace with population increase, although there are now—what with public health and reduction in the death rates—three times as many mouths to feed in the world as there were when Malthus's first essay appeared in 1824.

Malthus was right about restraint (using "restraint" in

a broad sense, to include family planning and contraceptive devices), but he was in error in believing that the threat of poverty or the fear of marginal living would induce restraint. The contrary proved to be true—the more abysmal the poverty, the higher the birth rate.

Malthus was likewise correct in believing that size of population and rate of population growth are major obstacles to improved living conditions. Moreover, the statistics of the last few years demonstrate that even with the miracles of technology, and with mechanization squeezing the ultimate radish out of the acre, and with pharmacists working twenty-four hours a day producing the Pill, the situation is rapidly getting out of control, with congestion threatening to choke humanity out of existence, if indeed the nuclear bomb does not first demolish the planet.

Latin America now occupies first place in the race toward population disaster, with a rate of increase of almost three percent a year, approximately double that of the United States or Russia. Asia and India, with a gigantic base to start from, are already outstripping home-grown foodstuffs.

In the United States itself, the toll of over-population is recorded in polluted lakes and rivers, ineradicable slums in every city, clogged highways, suffocation in the air, and the extinction of wildlife in the dwindling fields and forests of what less than two hundred years ago was a virgin continent, ripe for "civilization." Less than ten million Americans in 1800 have become over two hundred million, and there may be half as many again before the year 2000.

Population and peace. The nuclear bomb or the fertility bomb. Those are the challenges as the United States approaches the bicentennial of its independence, and those are the problems that face the world as it moves toward the 21st century. Everything else is subordinate. Nothing else is compelling. Unless mankind can find a way to live without recourse to nuclear war, before terrestrial congestion presses humanity back into the swamps and the oceans, international relations will cease to be of concern. The anatomy of diplomacy will be revealed as a desiccated skeleton, because nations will have ceased to matter.

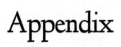

Appendix

PRESIDENT KENNEDY TO CHIEFS OF MISSION, MAY 29, 1961 [1]

DEAR MR. AMBASSADOR: Please accept my best wishes for the successful accomplishment of your mission. As the personal representative of the President of the United States in Greece, you are part of a memorable tradition which began with Benjamin Franklin and Thomas Jefferson, and which has included many of our most distinguished citizens.

We are living in a critical moment in history. Powerful destructive forces are challenging the universal values which, for centuries, have inspired men of good will in all parts of the world.

If we are to make progress toward a prosperous community of nations in a world of peace, the United States must exercise the most affirmative and responsible leadership. Beyond our shores, this leadership, in large measure, must be provided by our ambassadors and their staffs.

I have asked you to represent our Government in Greece because I am confident that you have the ability, dedication, and experience. The purpose of this letter is to define guidelines which I hope may be helpful to you.

The practice of modern diplomacy requires a close understanding not only of governments but also of people, their cultures and institutions. Therefore, I hope that you will plan your work so that you may have the time to travel extensively outside the nation's capital. Only in this way can you develop the close, personal associations that go beyond official diplomatic circles and maintain a sympathetic and accurate understanding of all segments of the country.

Moreover, the improved understanding which is so essential to a more peaceful and rational world is a two-way street. It is

---

[1] Paragraphs 16 and 17 were omitted from the letters sent to Ambassadors in countries in which there were no United States military forces under an area military commander.

our task not only to understand what motivates others, but to give them a better understanding of what motivates us.

Many persons in Greece who have never visited the United States, receive their principal impressions of our nation through their contact with Americans who come to their country either as private citizens or as government employees.

Therefore, the manner in which you and your staff personally conduct yourselves is of the utmost importance. This applies to the way in which you carry out your official duties and to the attitudes you and they bring to day-to-day contacts and associations.

It is an essential part of your task to create a climate of dignified, dedicated understanding, cooperation, and service in and around the Embassy.

In regard to your personal authority and responsibility, I shall count on you to oversee and coordinate all the activities of the United States Government in Greece.

You are in charge of the entire United States Diplomatic Mission, and I shall expect you to supervise all of its operations. The Mission includes not only the personnel of the Department of State and the Foreign Service, but also the representatives of all other United States agencies which have programs or activities in Greece. I shall give you full support and backing in carrying out your assignment.

Needless to say, the representatives of other agencies are expected to communicate directly with their offices here in Washington, and in the event of a decision by you in which they do not concur, they may ask to have the decision reviewed by a higher authority in Washington.

However, it is their responsibility to keep you fully informed of their views and activities and to abide by your decisions unless in some particular instance you and they are notified to the contrary.

If in your judgment individual members of the Mission are not functioning effectively, you should take whatever action you feel may be required, reporting the circumstances, of course, to the Department of State.

In case the departure from Greece of any individual member of the Mission is indicated in your judgment, I shall expect you to make the decision and see that it is carried into effect. Such instances I am confident will be rare.

Now one word about your relations to the military. As you know, the United States Diplomatic Mission includes Service Attachés, Military Assistance Advisory Groups and other Military components attached to the Mission. It does not, however, include United States military forces operating in the field where such forces are under the command of a United States area military commander. The line of authority to these forces runs from me, to the Secretary of Defense, to the Joint Chiefs of Staff in Washington and to the area commander in the field.

Although this means that the chief of the American Diplomatic Mission is not in the line of military command, nevertheless, as Chief of Mission, you should work closely with the appropriate area military commander to assure the full exchange of information. If it is your opinion that activities by the United States military forces may adversely affect our over-all relations with the people or government of Greece, you should promptly discuss the matter with the military commander and, if necessary, request a decision by higher authority.

I have informed all heads of departments and agencies of the Government of the responsibilities of the chiefs of American Diplomatic Missions for our combined operations abroad, and I have asked them to instruct their representatives in the field accordingly.

As you know, your own lines of communication as Chief of Mission run through the Department of State.

Let me close with an expression of confidence in you personally and the earnest hope that your efforts may help strengthen our relations with both the Government and the people of Greece. I am sure that you will make a major contribution to the cause of world peace and understanding.

Good luck and my warmest regards,

    Sincerely,

                (Signed)   JOHN F. KENNEDY

OFFICE OF DEPUTY UNDER SECRETARY FOR ADMINISTRATION

FOREIGN SERVICE INSTITUTE	BUREAU OF SECURITY AND CONSULAR AFFAIRS	OFFICE OF SECURITY	OFFICE OF COMMUNICATIONS	CONGRESSIONAL RELATIONS (APPROPRIATIONS)
GEORGE V. ALLEN	PHILIP B. HEYMANN (Acting)	G. MARVIN GENTILE	RICHARD P. SCOTT	WILLIAM R. LITTLE

EDWIN M. ADAMS	RALPH S. ROBERTS	JOHN M. STEEVES	W. O. TRONE	RICHARD W. BARRETT
SPECIAL PROGRAMS	BUDGET AND COMPLIANCE	DIRECTOR GENERAL	OPERATIONS	MANAGEMENT PLANNING
EXECUTIVE SECRETARIAT	FOREIGN SERVICE INSPECTION CORPS	BOARD OF EXAMINERS OF THE FOREIGN SERVICE	OFFICE OF OPERATIONS	CENTER FOR INTERNATIONAL SYSTEMS RESEARCH
EXECUTIVE DIRECTOR FOR ADMINISTRATION	AUDIT PROGRAM	EMPLOYMENT PROGRAM	ALLOWANCES PROGRAM	SUBSTANTIVE INFORMATION SYSTEMS PROGRAM
POLICY AND PUBLIC INFORMATION AFFAIRS PROGRAM	APPRAISALS AND PROGRAM ANALYSIS	JUNIOR OFFICER PROGRAM	COMMISSARY AND RECREATION PROGRAM	ORGANIZATIONAL STUDIES AND PROCEDURES PROGRAM
EQUAL EMPLOYMENT PRACTICES	BUDGET PLANNING AND PRESENTATION	MID CAREER OFFICER PROGRAM	OFFICE OF OVERSEAS SCHOOLS	MANAGEMENT SUGGESTIONS AND CONSULTATION PROGRAM
ADMINISTRATIVE AFFAIRS	FUNDS MANAGEMENT	SENIOR OFFICER PROGRAM	ART IN EMBASSIES PROGRAM	MANPOWER PLANNING PROGRAM
SPECIAL REVIEW PANEL	FINANCIAL MANAGEMENT SYSTEMS PROGRAM	STAFF SUPPORT PERSONNEL PROGRAM	OFFICE OF FOREIGN BUILDINGS	FAPS DEVELOPMENT PROGRAM
COMMUNITY ADVISORY SERVICES	MANAGEMENT REPORTS	FUNCTIONAL PERSONNEL PROGRAM	BUILDINGS DESIGN AND CONSTRUCTION PROGRAM	ACORD PROGRAM
RETIRED OFFICERS PROGRAM	INTERDEPARTMENTAL RELATIONS AND GAO LIAISON	LOCAL PERSONNEL PROGRAM	INTERIOR DESIGN AND FURNISHING PROGRAM	
		MEDICAL PROGRAM		
		PERFORMANCE EVALUATION		
		FOREIGN AFFAIRS TRAINING		
		EMPLOYEE RELATIONS		
		PRESIDENTIAL APPOINTMENTS		
		FOREIGN AFFAIRS PERSONNEL PLANNING		
		COLLEGE RELATIONS PROGRAM		

Foreign Affairs Manual Circular No. 430, dated July 25, 1966, is quoted below:

1. *Purpose*

Effective immediately, the Office of the Deputy Under Secretary for Administration is expanded to include an Executive Group which will assist in managing the "O" Area.

2. *Organization*

In addition to the Deputy Under Secretary, regular members of the Group are the Director General of the Foreign Service, the Deputy Assistant Secretary for Budget, the Directors of the Office of Management Planning and Office of Operations, and the Assistant for Special Programs. Other members who will participate on an ad hoc basis are the Director of the Foreign Service Institute, the Administrator of the Bureau of Security and Consular Affairs, the Deputy Assistant Secretary for Security, the Deputy Assistant Secretary for Communications, and the Special Assistant for Congressional Relations (Appropriations).

An Executive Secretariat is also established to support the operations of the Group.

Managers of independent administrative programs will continue to report to the Office of the Deputy Under Secretary for Administration.

To facilitate and strengthen the operations of the Office of Deputy Under Secretary, limited adjustments have been made in the current grouping of administrative programs (see attached chart).

3. *Manual Codification and Changes*

This circular supersedes those portions of FAMCs 311A, 326, 357, and 370 which may conflict with the contents of this circular. The circular will be cancelled six months from date of issue unless cancelled earlier as a result of codification in the Foreign Affairs Manual.

Following is the substantive portion of a letter dated May 5, 1965, from the author to Ambassador Raymond L. Thurston, then State Department Deputy at the Air War College, Montgomery, Alabama.

Dear Ray:

As you surmised, I have some doubts about the validity of the thesis that bigger and better education for more and more public servants would be a Good Thing; on the contrary, I am inclined to conclude that it would be a Bad Thing. It is my belief that bigger and better in-service training would be superfluous for all except a fractional proportion of [Foreign Service] officers, and that nothing along the line of wholesale educational opportunities for bureaucrats ought to be attempted.

I was astonished at the extent of such education already available—through the Civil Service Commission, for instance, and if I were Monarch of All I Surveyed, my first act would probably be to dismantle at least three quarters of existing *public* facilities, seeking their return to the private academic fold, and the extermination of recalcitrants.

The Foreign Service Institute I would limit to the teaching of foreign language, plus a few simple orientation Courses on the Mechanics of Things (in contrast to the Theory of International Relations). In particular I would suppress all FSI "mid-career training" and "senior officers training." For the possible one-in-a-hundred mid-career officers, the applicable post-graduate training could be arranged at a private institution.

The notion of a great post-graduate National Academy along

the line of the Herter Committee recommendations, I view with downright horror, and I accordingly cheered loudly when Dean Acheson committed a nuisance on the project—from which, as far as I am informed, it has not recovered. As I think I remarked at the time, it would be more practical to sell the existing National War College to the State Department, which could readily be done by executive fiat changing the management. That possibly would not improve the place as an educational institution but it would at least give a few senior diplomats some elegant quarters beside the Potomac, thus catering to the quaint idea that in peacetime the Civilian Authority is Paramount.

Also, it seems to me that citing percentages of military versus civilian types receiving in-service education does not prove much, for the reason that when the nation is not at war the soldiers have nothing much to do except (a) march to and fro, or (b) study how the last war might more quickly have been lost.

As you know, I have supported the presence of top-ranking FSO's at war colleges, for the reasons you have cogently stated. But have we in fact maintained the caliber of those participants? It is my impression that we have not, and that many instances of the attendance of mediocre candidates could now be cited. Each dope impairs the efficiency of the arrangement.

Sincerely yours,
ELLIS BRIGGS

The Honorable Raymond L. Thurston
American Ambassador
Air University
Maxwell AFB, Alabama

Index

241